Computer Crafts for Kids

D1518555

Computer Crafts for Kids

Margy Kuntz and Ann Kuntz

ZIFF-DAVIS PRESS

EMERYVILLE, CALIFORNIA

Senior Development Editor
Melinda E. Levine

Copy Editor
Kelly Green

Technical Reviewer
Heidi Steele

Project Coordinator
Barbara Dahl

Proofreader
Carol Burbo

Cover Illustration
Carrie English and Cherie
Plumlee Computer Graphics
and Illustration

Cover Designer
Carrie English

Book Designer
John Sullivan/Visual Strategies,
San Francisco

Screen Graphics Editor
Dan Brodnitz

Technical Illustrator
Cherie Plumlee Computer
Graphics and Illustration

Word Processor
Howard Blechman

Layout Artist
Bruce Lundquist

Indexer
Valerie Robbins

Photographer
Ken Rice

Ziff-Davis Press books are produced on a Macintosh computer system with the following applications: FrameMaker®, Microsoft® Word, QuarkXPress®, Adobe Illustrator®, Adobe Photoshop®, Adobe Streamline™, MacLink®*Plus*, Aldus® FreeHand™, Collage Plus™.

Ziff-Davis Press
5903 Christie Avenue
Emeryville, CA 94608
1-800-688-0448

ISBN 1-56276-186-2

Manufactured in the United States of America
10 9 8 7 6 5 4 3 2 1

Acknowledgments

We would like to thank the great kids who helped us choose the projects:

Elliott Belser
Daniel Chelton
Allison Dierdorff
Elizabeth Dierdorff
Gene Fielden
Maggie Fielden
Emily Hone
James Thomas

We are also grateful to our husbands, Bob Hone and Tack Kuntz, who did not complain when our living rooms looked like art studios and who provided us with support throughout the whole process.

And thanks to all the folks at Ziff-Davis for their encouragement and enthusiasm.

Table of Contents

Introduction

For Parents and Teachers: About This Book

Welcome to *Computer Crafts for Kids,* a collection of exciting craft projects that can be created with Word for Windows 6.0. Why Word? Because we feel that children can and want to use "adult" programs; they just haven't been given a reason or an opportunity to use them. This book not only reveals many of the features of Word, but helps stimulate children to explore the creative side of computers.

The projects range from fun to functional, and simple to complex. Each guides the child through the process of first creating the computer output, and then using the output to assemble the final craft. Although some of the projects are progressive—building on tools and commands used previously—they have been designed so they can be done in any order.

To do the projects in this book, you should have the following: an IBM-compatible computer running Windows, Word for Windows 6.0, a mouse, a printer, and plain printer paper. Most of the materials used in the crafts are common household items, which are listed in the You'll Need section of each project. If you have the opportunity, you also might want to provide special items such as colored printer paper (available in most office supply, stationery, and general supply stores) and glitter glue sticks.

We hope your children will enjoy creating the projects in *Computer Crafts for Kids* as much as we did. And of course, feel free to try them, too!

Getting Started

In this part of the book, you'll find what you need to know about starting Word, opening and closing files, saving and printing projects, and more. If you already know how to do these things, jump right into the projects in the next part.

Starting Up

Before you get started, make sure that Word 6.0 for Windows is on your computer. You'll also need to know how to start Windows. If you need help, ask your folks or a teacher or a friend to show you how to run Windows and where to find Word for Windows on your computer. Then the rest is simple.

Starting a New Project

1 Find the Word 6.0 *icon* (an icon is a tiny picture). It looks like this:

Word 6.0 icon

Use the mouse to move the *pointer* (the little arrow) over the icon and double-click the left mouse button. That's all there is to it.

2 Look at the Word screen when it shows up.

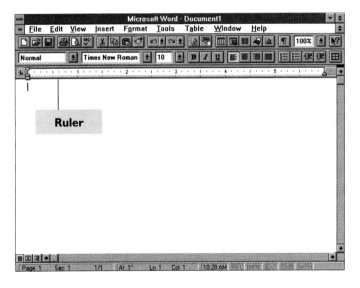

Ruler

When the Word screen first appears, you may see a small Tip of the Day box. To close the

Tip of the Day box, just click on the OK button in the box.

3 If you don't see the bar that looks like a ruler at the top of your screen, just click once on the *View menu* (it's called a menu because it gives you a bunch of things to choose from). Select Ruler from the list by clicking on it. Now you're ready to start.

Restarting a Saved Project

I To reopen a project you've already saved, first follow steps 1 and 2 above. Then click on the File menu (the first one on the left), and select the Open command. You'll see a box called the Open dialog box.

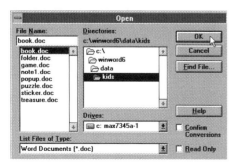

2 Find the name of the project you saved and click on it to select it. Then click on the OK button. Your project will open up so you can work on it again.

Changing the Paper Orientation

Sometimes you'll want your paper to be taller than it is wide (Word calls this *portrait* orientation), and other times you'll want it to be wider than it is tall (Word calls this *landscape* orientation). When you first open Word, the paper is always in the portrait setting. Here's how to tell Word that you want the orientation to be landscape instead.

Portrait orientation

Landscape orientation

First click on the File menu to see the list of choices. Then select Page Setup (it's the tenth choice down) by clicking on it. You'll see the Page Setup dialog box.

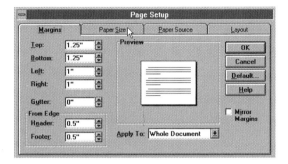

See the tabs near the top of the dialog box? Click on the tab that says Paper Size. Now you should see the Paper Size choices.

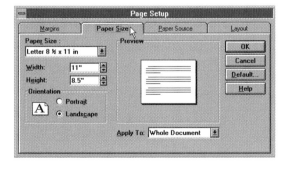

Now just click in the small Landscape circle. A black dot will show up in the circle.

If you decide you want your page to have portrait orientation after all, then just click in the small Portrait circle.

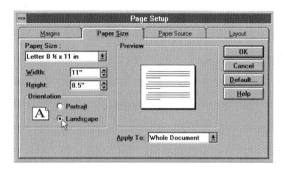

Next, click on the OK button to close the dialog box. Now you're ready to go!

Saving Your Files

You probably already know this, but if you don't save the project (or *file*) you've created, you'll lose it forever. So always be sure to save the things you want to keep—it's really easy to do!

Saving a New Project

Go to the File menu and click on it once. Then click on the Save command.

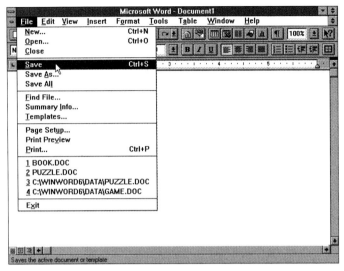

Choosing the Save command

(You could also try this shortcut: Just press the Ctrl key and S on the keyboard at the same time.)

2 Now, you'll see the Save As dialog box. See the box under the words File Name up at the top? Just use the keyboard to type the name of your project in that box.

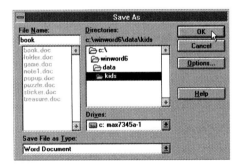

(Remember, the name can't have more than eight letters

or numbers.) Then click on the OK button. Now your project is saved.

Oh No!

A Message Asks If I Want to Replace an Existing File!

If your project has the same name as another saved project, then you'll see this message. The best thing to do is to click on the No button. Then type a new name in the File Name box. Don't forget to click on the OK button when you're done typing in the new name.

Saving Changes to a Saved File

This is really simple. Just select Save from the File menu, as you did in step 1 of Saving a New Project. Word will automatically save the changes for you.

Printing Tips

You'll need to print out words or drawings for each project in this book, so be sure that the printer is turned on and working correctly.

Basic Printing

1 When you're ready to print, click on the File menu, and select Print from the list of choices. (Or, you can just press the Ctrl key and P at the same time.) You'll see the Print dialog box, like this:

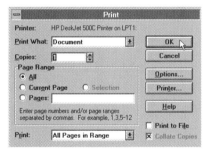

2 Now all you have to do is click on the OK button and wait for your project to print!

Using Print Preview

1 Print Preview lets you see what your page looks like before you print it. (This is really handy when you want to know if everything is going to fit on one page.) To use Print Preview, go to the File menu and select the Print Preview command. The Print Preview window will appear.

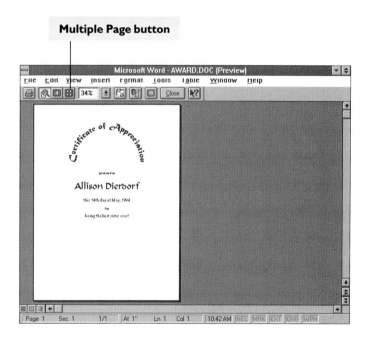

Everything that fits on a page will show up in the white space on the Print Preview window.

2 If you want to see more than one page at a time, click on the button that looks like four tiny pages in a gray box (it's called the *Multiple Page button*). Then, to pick the number of pages you want to see, hold down the mouse button, and drag the pointer over the page squares.

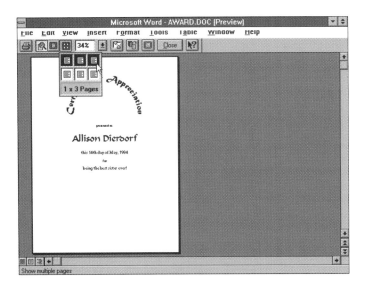

When you let go of the mouse button, the screen will change to show you more pages.

3 When you're done checking things out in Print Preview, just click on the Close button.

Closing Up

It's usually a good idea to close files when you're done using them. (Remember to save your project first!) Here's how.

To Close a Project

When you're finished with a project, click on the File menu. Then select Close. That's it!

Oh No!

A Message Asks If I Want to Save My File!

If you haven't saved before you close a project, you'll get this message. To save the project, just click on the Yes button. If you don't want to save it, click on the No button. (Clicking on the Cancel button tells Word that you decided not to close the project after all.)

To Exit Word

If you're finished using Word, go to the File menu and select the Exit command (it's the very last one). The Word window will close up.

Cool Craft Tricks

You'll find a lot of tricks for doing the projects in this book (keep an eye out for the Neat

Tricks and Try This boxes). But here are a few more tricks that will make your projects even better!

Trick 1: Quick Color

If you want a lot of color in your projects, try printing them on colored paper. You'll need special paper for your printer to do this (ask your folks or another adult about what papers to use). If you have the right paper, all you need to do is load up your printer and print away!

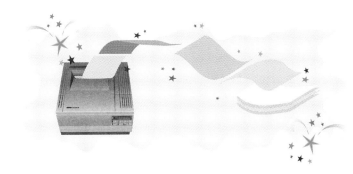

Trick 2: Coloring over Words

To color in your projects, try markers, crayons, colored pencils, even paint. But if you want to color over words, markers work best because they don't cover up the print.

Trick 3: No-Mess Gluing

Using a glue stick is one way to keep glue from getting all over the place. But here's another trick that will keep glue in its place. Instead of rubbing down a glued piece of art with your hands, first put a clean sheet of paper on top of the art. Then smooth the art down by rubbing on the clean sheet. This keeps the glue off your hands and your art work from smearing.

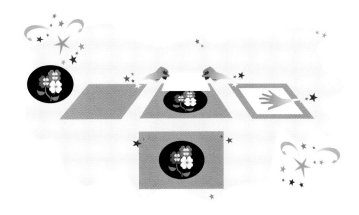

Trick 4: Putting on Glitter

You may want to use glitter to decorate some of your projects (we did!). But glitter can get all over the place. Here's how to put it exactly where you want it. Mix a little glue in a cup with a bit of water. Then use an old, clean paintbrush to brush the glue where you want the glitter to go. Shake on the glitter. Then lift up the page, holding it over another sheet of paper, and tap it to get rid of the extra glitter. (This trick works for confetti, too!)

And Now the Fun Begins!

PART 2

So now Word for Windows is running, and you're staring at a blank screen. What next? How about making placemats for a party, stickers for friends, secret messages with their own decoders, pop-up cards, pencil holders, and more! Just pick any project, and you're on your way!

Bumper Stickers

Bumper stickers aren't just for cars. Make up silly sayings to put on your notebooks, locker doors, even the fridge! (But don't put these on painted doors or walls—they'll pull up the paint.

MY OTHER CAR IS A BICYCLE

Go Giants!

PLEASE GIVE ANIMALS A BRAKE

SAVE the SNAILS

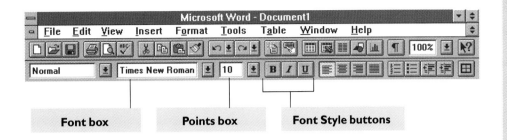

Font box   **Points box**   **Font Style buttons**

Here's How to Do It

You'll Need

- *scissors*
- *markers, crayons, or colored pencils (optional)*
- *clear contact paper*
- *ruler*
- *pencil*

1 Bumper stickers are short and wide, so the first thing you have to do is make your page short and wide. To do this, you need to change your page setup to Landscape. (If you don't know how to do this, see Changing the Paper Orientation, page 2.)

2 Make up a silly saying or slogan for your sticker, and type it in. Don't worry if you make a mistake, just use the Backspace key or Delete key to erase the letters.

3 Now we need to change the size of the letters, so they're big and easy to read. First, select a line of your slogan using the mouse. Next, find the box with the number in it—it's above the ruler. This box is called the *Points box*. Click once on the down arrow to the right of the box— a whole list of numbers will show up. To see more numbers, use the up and down arrows to move through the list. Then click on a number to choose it. For big letters, pick a big number, such as 48.

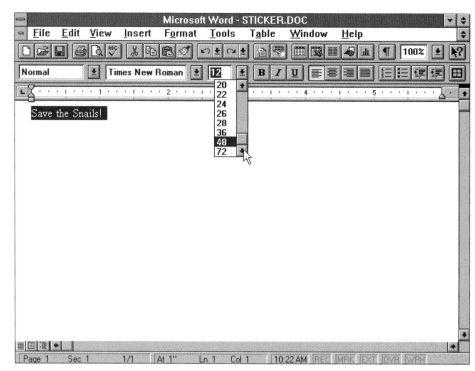

The Points box

Oh No!

My Words Don't Stay on One Line!

If you want your words to stay on one line, try using a smaller number for the point size.

4 Now let's change the way the letters look by changing the typeface (called the *font*). Select your words using the mouse. Then click on the down arrow next to the *Font box* (it's to the left of the Points box). A list of different font names drops down. Select one. If you don't like the font you picked, just make sure your words are still selected, then pick a different font using the Font box.

5 You can also use the three Font Style buttons to change the way your bumper sticker looks. Select the words you want to change. Then try clicking on the B, I, and U buttons. The B button makes letters thicker and darker (called *bold*), the I button makes letters slanted (called *italic*), and the U button underlines the letters (look at the top of the next page for examples).

Bold   *Italic*   Underline

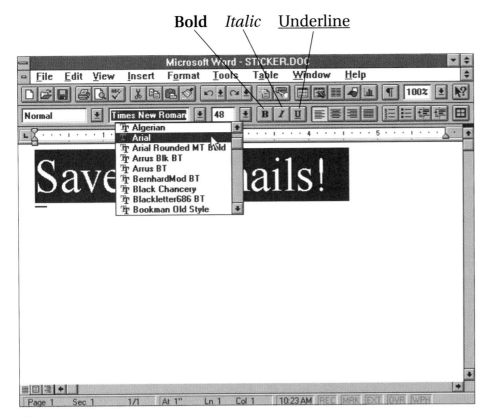

The Font box

If you change your mind about a font style, press the Font Style button again to turn it off. Play around until you like your sticker. Then save it using the Save command (see Saving Your Files, page 3).

6 Print out your bumper sticker. You might try using colored printer paper if you have it. (If you forget how to print, see Printing Tips, page 5) Fold the sheet with your bumper sticker slogan on it in half the long way. Cut along the fold. If you want, add colored decorations or pictures to the bumper sticker.

7 Now let's make the sticker sticky. Use a ruler and a pencil to draw a box on the contact paper. The box should be 5½ inches wide and 12 inches long. Cut out the box.

Neat Trick

If you want your slogan to be centered on the page, select all the words and then press the Ctrl key and E at the same time. If you don't want the text centered, press the Ctrl key and L together.

Oh No!

My Words Get Cut Off When I Fold the Page!

If your words don't fit when you fold the printed page in half, open up your saved file, select all the text, and then pick a smaller number for the point size. Print out the new bumper sticker.

Try This

If you have sticker paper for your printer, print out your bumper sticker using the sticker paper. Then all you have to do fold the paper in half lengthwise and cut along the fold. Peel off the backing, and put up your sticker!

8 Place the piece of contact paper with the clear side down on a clean hard surface. Carefully peel off the backing—but don't throw it away, you'll use it again later.

9 Hold your bumper sticker page with the word side down so that it's a little above the contact paper. Make sure it's centered so there's about the same amount of space on each side. Slowly lower the slogan down so it touches the contact paper a bit at a time, starting with one side. Smooth it as you go.

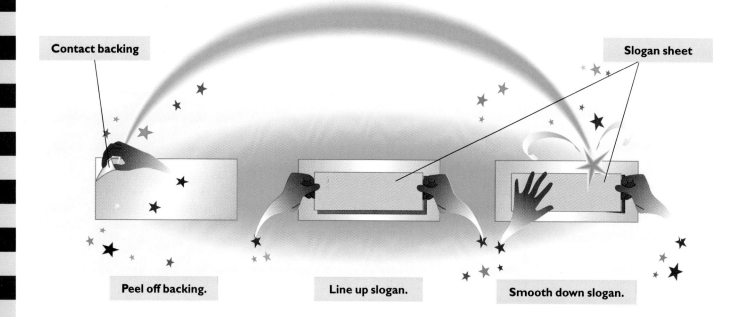

Contact backing

Slogan sheet

Peel off backing.

Line up slogan.

Smooth down slogan.

10 Take the piece of backing that you peeled off and put it back on over the sticky edges of the contact paper. Try to line up the edges so all of the sticky surface is covered.

11 When you've decided where you want your bumper sticker to go, just peel off the backing and press around the edges.

Party Placemats

These colorful placemats are great for any type of celebration—make them for birthdays, holidays, or just-because parties.

Ben's Birthday

Let's all celebrate
Dance and sing
Run, jump, and play.
For Ben was born today!

Happy Birthday!

B IS FOR BIRTHDAY

Once there was a little boy named Ben. Ben wanted a bunny for his birthday. He got a baseball and a bat and a book, but no ... Ben felt bad. Then his brother told him to go in the ... There in a big box under a bush was a black and white ... the best birthday.

FUN THINGS TO DO ON THE FOURTH OF JULY!

1. Wear red, white & blue.
2. Have a picnic.
3. Go to a parade.
4. Have fun with friends.
5. Watch fireworks.

In the U.S.A
the Fourth of July
is our country's birthday.
So give three cheers,
hip, hip, hooray!

The Declaration of Independence, July 4 1776

"We hold these truths to be self-evident, that all men are created equal, that they are endowed by their Creator with certain inalienable Rights, that among these are Life, Liberty and the Pursuit of Happiness..."

On the Menu

Alignment buttons

You'll Need

- *ruler*
- *compass*
- *pencil*
- *scissors*
- *colored paper or wrapping paper*
- *glue stick or glue*
- *11-by-14-inch poster board, any color*
- *decorations such as ribbons, stickers, glitter, and confetti*
- *clear contact paper*

Here's How to Do It

1 What kind of party are your placemats for? A birthday? Fourth of July? Thanksgiving? Find or write two or three short poems, songs, or stories about the day. Type each one. (You can start a new line by pressing the Enter or Return key.) Then press the Enter key or Return key six or seven times after each poem, song, or story.

2 If you want, change the typeface (called the font in Word for Windows) and/or the size of the letters (the point size). Just use your mouse to select the words you want to change. Then use the Font box and the Points box. Click on the arrow next to each box and scroll through the lists to pick the font and size you like. (For more about changing the size and style of your words, see the Bumper Stickers project.)

3 Now, let's change the way the lines of text line up—this is called *alignment*. You can make all the text lines centered. You can make all the text lines even on the right side (called *right aligned*). You can make all the text lines

even on both sides (called *justified*). Or you can keep the lines of text as they are, so they are even on the left side (*left aligned*).

This example shows
lines of text that
are centered.

This example shows
lines of text that
are right aligned.

This example shows
lines of text that are
justified just like this.

This example shows
lines of text that
are left aligned.

To change the alignment, you use (surprise!) the Alignment buttons. See how each button looks like a tiny version of the way the text lines up? Use the mouse to select one of the poems, songs, or stories that you wrote, then click on one of the Alignment buttons. If you don't like the way the text looks, then click on another Alignment button. Choose an alignment for each different poem, song, or story.

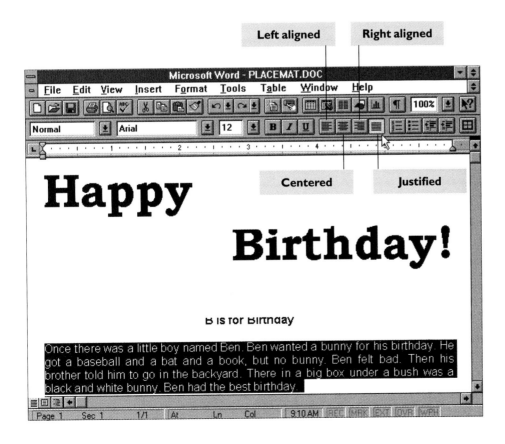

4 When you're done, save your project using the Save command. Then print out the page(s).(For more about saving and printing, see Saving Your Files, page 3, and Printing Tips, page 5.)

5 Use your ruler or compass and a pencil to draw a box or circle around each poem, song, or story that you printed. Cut out the shapes.

6 Pick some colorful papers to use as frames. Try fancy gift wrap if you're making a birthday mat, or maybe red, white, and blue papers for a Fourth of July mat. Glue each of the shapes you cut out onto the paper and let it dry. Then use your ruler or compass to draw another box or circle around each shape, leaving enough of the colored paper or wrapping paper showing to make a frame. Cut out the framed pieces.

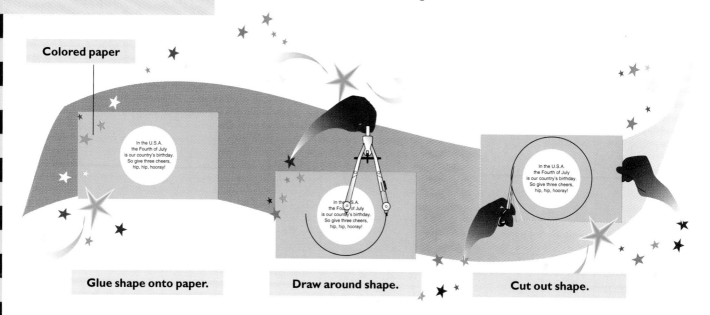

Colored paper

In the U.S.A. the Fourth of July is our country's birthday. So give three cheers, hip, hip, hooray!

In the U.S.A. the Fourth of July is our country's birthday. So give three cheers, hip, hip, hooray!

In the U.S.A. the Fourth of July is our country's birthday. So give three cheers, hip, hip, hooray!

Glue shape onto paper.   **Draw around shape.**   **Cut out shape.**

7 Place your framed pieces on the poster board in an interesting pattern. Add bits of ribbon, stickers, and other decorations that will

press down flat—bows with knots in them, heavy cords or yarn, and curled-up ribbon won't work. Finish up with confetti or glitter.

When you're happy with the placemat, glue down your shapes and decorations. Really small stuff—such as confetti—can be left unpasted.

8 Now you're going to make your placemat waterproof. Cut two 1-by-1½-foot pieces of contact paper. If your pieces are curling a lot, roll them up the opposite way from the curl to straighten them out.

Put one sheet of the contact paper, with the clear side down, on a hard surface, and peel off

Try This

Here's how to make your own color-coordinated confetti. Cut out several very thin strips of paper or foil. Hold the strips in a tight bundle over the poster board and cut across the ends to make tiny squares. Or use a hole puncher to make dots.

Oh No!

There Are Air Bubbles in My Placemat!

First try smoothing the contact paper very firmly with your hand, pushing the bubbles toward the edges. To get rid of stubborn bubbles, make a tiny hole with a pin in the center of a bubble—just a little prick will do—and rub out the bubble with your thumbnail.

the backing. Pick up your mat carefully, keeping it level so the unglued pieces don't move around, and place it on the contact paper. Leave some space all around the placemat, but you don't have to center it perfectly on the contact paper.

9 Start to peel the backing off of one corner of the second sheet of contact paper. Line it up with a corner of the first piece. Smooth it down, and slowly peel off the rest of the backing a bit at a time. Smooth it over the placemat as you go.

10 When the contact paper is tight and smooth on both sides of the placemat, run your thumbnail around the edge of the poster board to make sure the edges are sealed together. Then trim off the extra contact paper that sticks out from the edges of the poster board. Now, make some more for other people at the party!

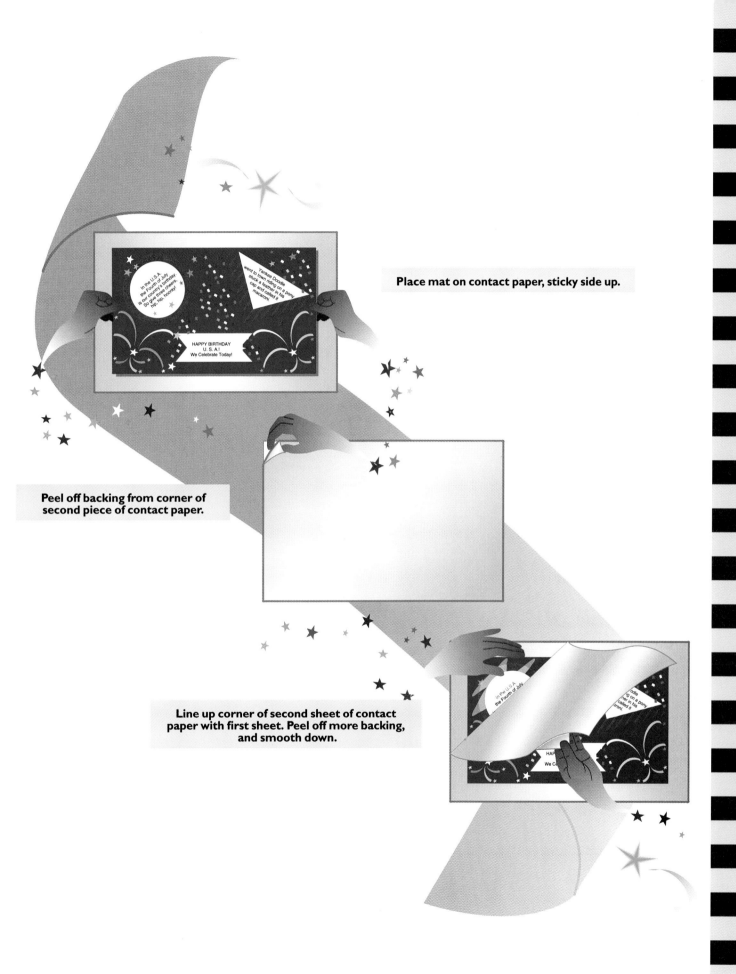

Place mat on contact paper, sticky side up.

In the U.S.A.
the Fourth of July
is our country's birthday.
So give three cheers,
hip, hip, hooray!

Yankee Doodle
went to town riding on a pony
stuck a feather in his
cap and called it
macaroni.

HAPPY BIRTHDAY
U. S. A!
We Celebrate Today!

**Peel off backing from corner of
second piece of contact paper.**

**Line up corner of second sheet of contact
paper with first sheet. Peel off more backing,
and smooth down.**

Super Secret Messages

Psst.... Want to give your friend a message that no one else can read? Word for Windows makes it easy. First you'll code a message, then you'll make a decoder so your friend can read the message.

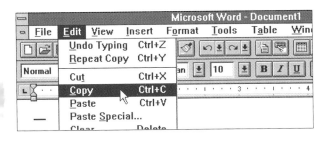

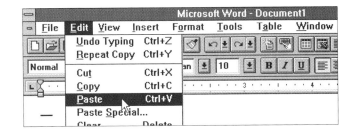

Here's How to Do It

Type in a message that you would like to send to a friend. Now here's where the secret part comes in. Select your whole message. Then click once on the arrow to the right of the Font box. When the list of fonts drops down, select Symbol.

- *scissors*
- *glue stick or glue*
- *empty toilet paper roll*
- *ruler*
- *pencil*
- *markers*
- *transparent tape*

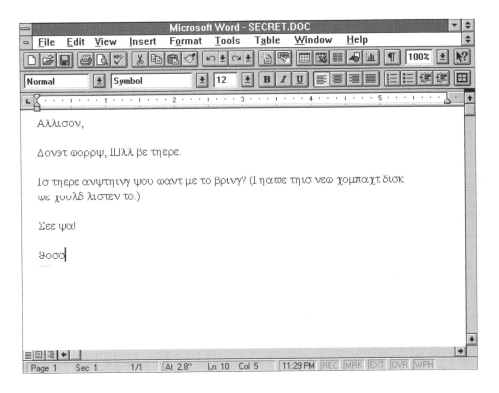

Your message will change into strange-looking characters! Save it, then print it out. (For more on saving and printing, see Saving Your Files, page 3 and Printing Tips, page 5.)

2 Now we'll start on the decoder. The decoder lets your friend know what letter each symbol represents. Select New from the File menu, then click on the OK button to bring up a fresh page. First we need to make the page print lengthwise. To do this, you need to change your page setup to Landscape. (If you don't know how to do this, see Changing the Paper Orientation, page 2.)

3 Type in the letter *a*, then press the Tab key. See how the blinking line (called the *insertion point*) moves to the right? Now type in the letter *b* and press the Tab key again. Continue typing in the letters of the alphabet, through *i*. Remember to press the Tab key between each letter. Then hit the Enter or Return key three times.

Next, type in the letters *j* through *r*, hitting the Tab key between each letter. Then press the Enter or Return key three times again. Finally, type the letters *s* through *z* the same way. Press the Enter or Return key once or twice after you type the *z*.

4 Select the first line of letters (*a* to *i*). Then select the Copy command from the Edit menu.

Now press the down arrow key once to move the insertion point down one line. Select the Paste command from the Edit menu. (It's right under the Copy command.) A second row of letters, from *a* to *i*, appears. Repeat these steps for each

Neat Trick

You don't have to Copy and Paste from the menus if you don't want to. You can use the keyboard instead. Just press the Ctrl key and C at the same time to copy, or press the Ctrl key and V at the same time to paste.

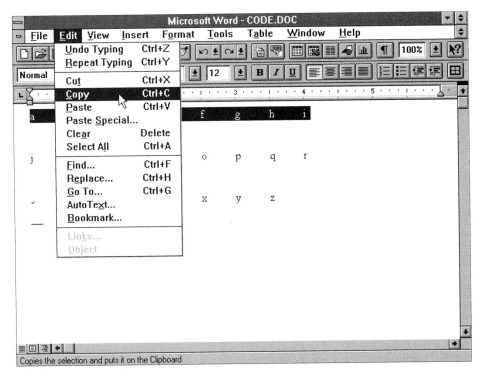

The Copy command

of the lines of letters. You now have three sets of letters—each set has two identical lines.

5 Go back to the first line and select it. Change the font to Symbol, as you did in step 1. You've just finished the first line of your decoder!

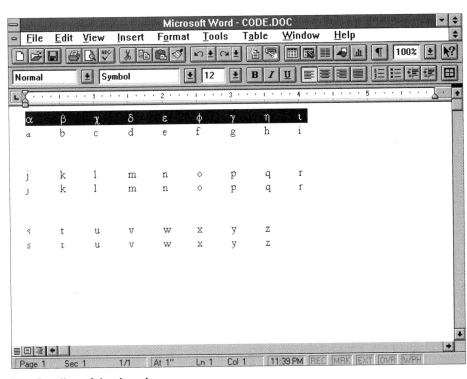

The first line of the decoder

Change the font to Symbol for the first line in each of the other two sets of letters, *j* through *r* and *s* through *z*.

6 Save and print your decoder sheet.

7 Fold your printout in half lengthwise. Then fold it in half again, across.

Fold lengthwise.

Then fold across.

Open up the paper and cut along the folds. Your code will be on one of the four pieces of paper. Take that piece and glue it tightly around the toilet paper roll with the print side showing. Make sure the top edge is lined up with the top of the toilet paper roll. (If there is extra paper along the bottom of the toilet paper roll, trim it off.)

8 Take one of the leftover sheets and fold it in half across. Use a ruler and a pencil to make a little pencil mark on the folded edge ½ inch from the top. Make another pencil mark ½ inch from the bottom.

Using the ruler, make a line ⅛ inch long, straight in from the edge of the paper at each mark. Then draw another line that connects the first two. Cut out carefully along the lines, and then unfold the sheet. There will be a window in the paper.

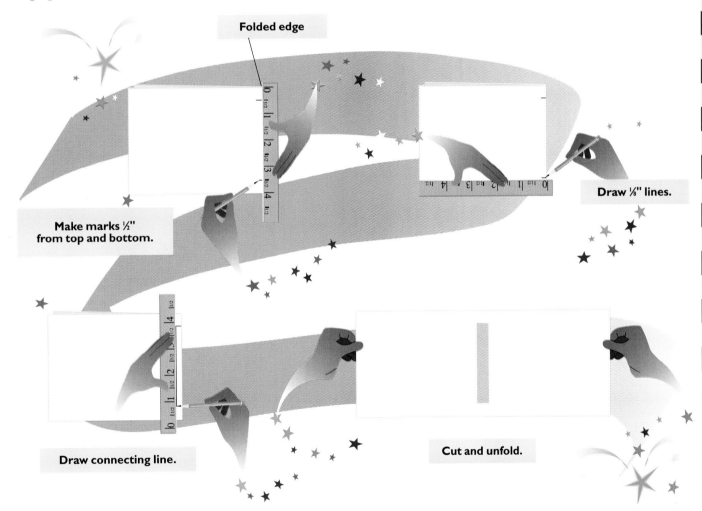

Folded edge

Make marks ½" from top and bottom.

Draw ⅛" lines.

Draw connecting line.

Cut and unfold.

9 Make a colorful design on the paper that has the window. (If you don't like your first design, use another one of the leftover pieces of paper, make a window in it, and try again.)

When your design is done, wrap the paper around the decoder. Line up the edges at the top of the roll. Make it just loose enough to turn but not so loose that it will fall off. Then tape the paper together from top to bottom where it overlaps.

Back

Front

Try This

To make the decoder easy to carry, put the roll on a long piece of string and knot the ends together. Then you can hang it over your shoulder. You can also roll up your secret message and store it inside the decoder.

You should be able to see three sets of letters through the window. As you turn the top sheet, the window will show different sets of coded letters. Give your friend the secret message and the decoder so he or she can decipher your message.

Dandy Doorknob Hangers

Wen Fu's Room

PLEASE

come in

stay out

Please!

Do Not Disturb

message from Maria

— I am —

sleeping
studying
AVAILABLE
back soon
hungry

What's a friendly way to tell people that you're busy studying or that they can come on in and talk? Just put one of these doorknob hangers on your door!

On the Menu

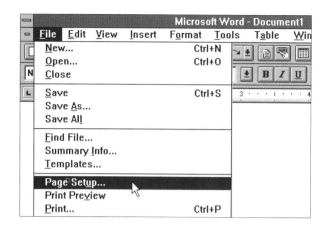

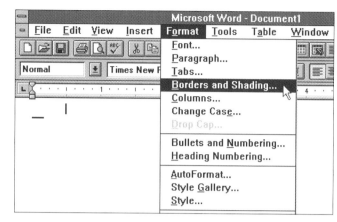

You'll Need

- *glue*
- *ruler*
- *pencil*
- *compass*
- *scissors*
- *markers, colored pencils, or crayons (optional)*

Here's How to Do It

Doorknob hangers need to be narrow so they don't get caught in the door. They also need to have room at the top for the doorknob hole. It's easy to make them fit by changing the margins of the page. To do this, first pull down the File menu and select the Page Setup command (it's ten down from the top). You should see a box like this one:

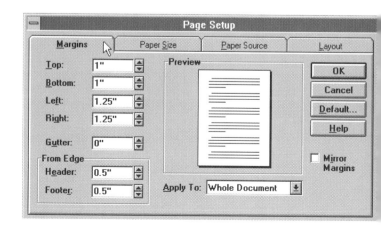

If you don't see this box, look for the four tabs under Page Setup. Click on the first tab—Margins. Now you should see the dialog box.

2 Find the box next to the word *Top*. Select the number in the box and press the Backspace key or the Delete key to erase the number. Now type **4** in the box.

Next, select the number in the box next to the word *Left* and press the Backspace key or the Delete key to erase it. Type **.5** into the box. Don't forget the decimal point (use a period) before the 5. Now, select the number in the box next to the word *Right* and press the Backspace key or the Delete key again. Type **4.75** into the box. This is what the margin numbers should look like:

Top:	4	
Bottom:	1"	
Left:	.5	
Right:	4.75	

Click on the OK button.

3 Now type in the words for your hanger. The hanger could be as simple as "Do Not Disturb," or it could be several lines long. If you want different words on different lines, press the Enter or Return key after each group of words that you want to keep together.

4 If you want, change the typeface (font), the size (point size), and the alignment of the text. (If you don't know how to do these things, see the Bumper Stickers and Party Placemats projects.)

Neat Trick

To quickly select the numbers in one of the white boxes, just move the pointer over the box and double-click the mouse button. You can also click on the up and down arrows next to the boxes to make the numbers larger or smaller.

5 Now let's make the doorknob hanger look really neat by adding a border around your words. Select the words that you want to put a border around, then pull down the Format menu and select the Borders and Shading command. A dialog box will show up. Click on the Borders tab at the top of the dialog box. You'll see a dialog box that looks like this one:

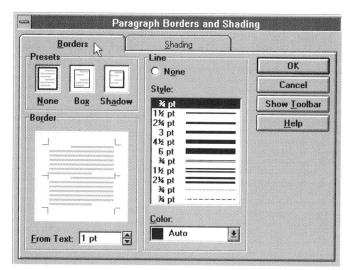

6 See the three white boxes near the top of the dialog box? Click on the middle one. Then click on one of the lines under the word *Style* on the right side. You'll see what your border will look like in the Border box on the left side. Try clicking on different lines to find the one you like best, then click on the OK button. Your words now have a border around them!

7 If you want to make your hanger even fancier, you can add a pattern inside the border. To do this, make sure your text is still selected, then select Borders and Shading from the Format menu again. Then click on the Shading tab at the top of the dialog box. You'll see a new dialog box with a bunch of different patterns in the middle, like this:

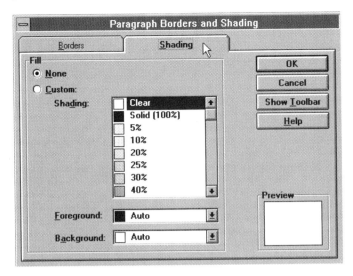

8 Click on the up and down arrows to move through the list of patterns until you find a pattern that you like. Click on the pattern, then click on the OK button. You'll see your pattern inside the border. Play around with different patterns and lines until you get a combination you like.

9 Save your doorknob hanger design and then print it out. (If you need to know more about saving and printing, see Saving Your Files, page 3, and Printing Tips, page 5.)

Fold the printed sheet in half lengthwise, making sure your words are on the outside of the fold. Glue the inside halves of the folded paper together.

10 Measure 4 inches down the side from each top corner and make a little dot with a pencil. Using the ruler, make a big *X* by drawing a line from each top corner to the dot on the opposite side.

Try This

If your doorknob hanger has several messages (Sleeping, Studying, Time to Talk, Not Here, etc.), use a brightly colored paper clip to point to the right message.

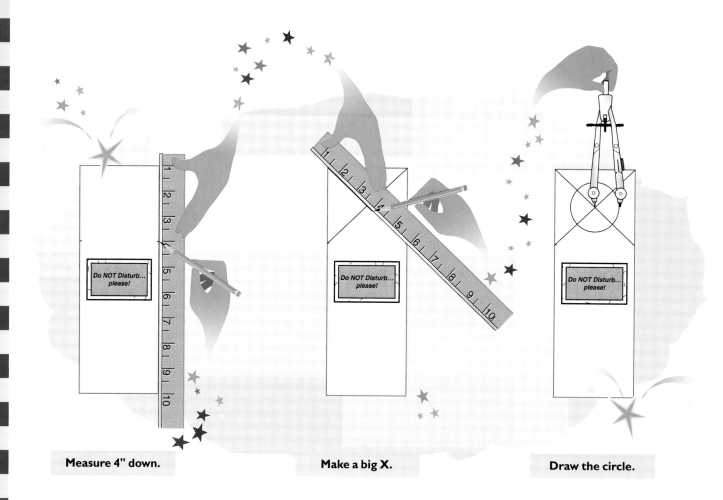

Measure 4" down.

Make a big X.

Draw the circle.

Neat Trick

If you don't have a compass, you can make one using a pencil and string. Tie a piece of string onto the pencil, near the point. Measure 1 inch from the center along one line of the X and make a mark. Put the pencil point on the mark. Hold down the string on the center of the X with your finger or a tack. Move the pencil in a circle around your finger or the tack (keep the string pulled tight).

Set the metal leg of the compass at the 1-inch mark. Then place the point of your compass at the center of the X, and draw a circle.

|| Cut along one of the lower lines of the X to the edge of the circle, and then cut out the circle. Carefully erase any leftover lines. Add color or decoration if you want, and your doorknob hanger is ready to swing.

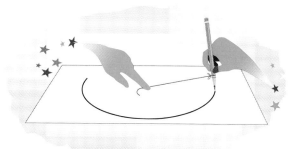

Amazing Awards

Certificate of Appreciation

presented to

Allison Dierdorf

this 14th day of May, 1994

for

being the best sister ever!

Friend for Life

This special award is for

Tom Ikinicapi

from his best friend

Jules Blackburn   *June 11, 1994*

PRESENTED TO GENE FIELDEN
FEBRUARY 1, 1994

Has someone in your life done something special? Make him or her a great award, with its own folder! (To make these awards extra fancy, try decorating the folder with silver or gold foil.)

On the Menu

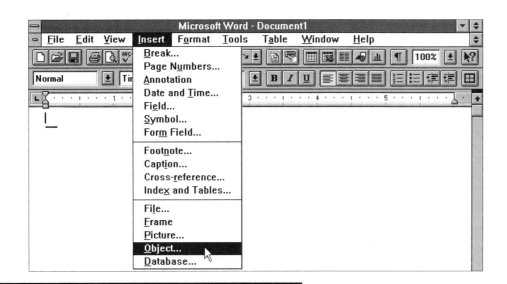

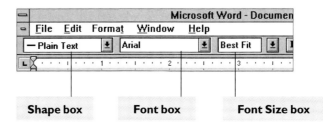

Shape box   **Font box**   **Font Size box**

Update Display

Update Display button

You'll Need

- *Two 12-by-18-inch pieces of colored construction paper*
- *pencil*
- *ruler*
- *scissors*
- *glue stick or glue*
- *markers, crayons, or colored pencils*
- *compass or small circular object (optional)*
- *certificate seals or foil or foil paper (optional)*

Continued on next page.

Here's How to Do It

1 To make your award wider than it is long, you first need to change your page setup to Landscape. (If you don't know how to do this, see Changing the Paper Orientation, page 2.)

2 Decide what kind of award you want to give. Will it be a Certificate of Merit? Or maybe a Gold Medal award? Or even a Friend (or Teacher) of the Year award? We're going to make the name of the award fancy using a special feature called WordArt 2.0, so don't type in your ideas yet. Instead, go to the Insert menu and select the second-to-last command—the Object command. A box (called a *dialog box*) will appear on the screen.

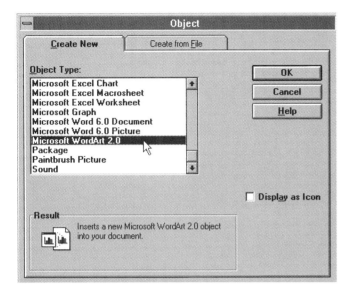

You'll Need

(continued)

- **short pieces of ribbon (optional)**
- **WordArt 2.0 (this program comes with Word for Windows; if WordArt 2.0 is not present, ask a grown-up to use the Word for Windows disks to install it)**

3 Click on the tab with the words *Create New* at the top of the dialog box. If you need to, use the up and down arrows to find the name *Microsoft WordArt 2.0*. Click on the name, then click on the OK button.

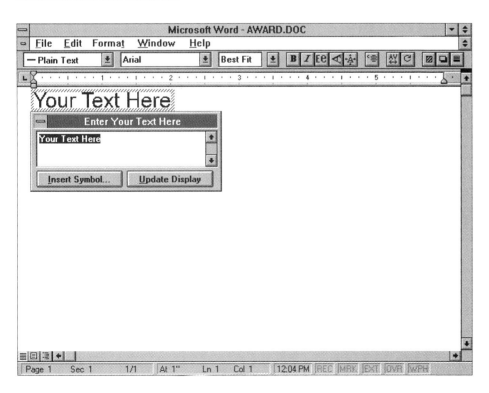

If you want more than one line for your award name, press the Enter or Return key after the last word in the first line, then start typing in the second line.

4 The first thing you need to do is type in the name of your award. Somewhere in the WordArt window you'll see a mini-window that says *Enter Your Text Here.* Inside the mini-window, you'll see the words *Your Text Here.* Start typing in the award name. The words *Your Text Here* should erase when you start to type. (If they don't, use the Backspace or Delete key to erase them.)

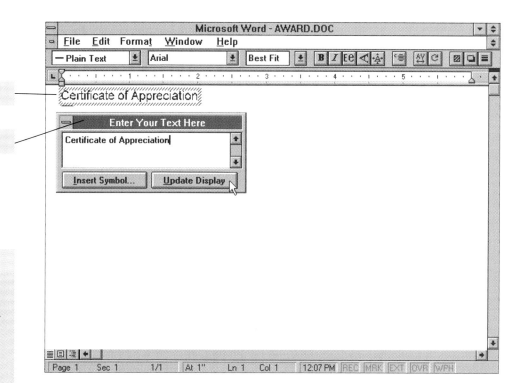

WordArt box

Mini-window

Oh No!

I Want to Change My Words and I've Already Clicked on the Update Display Button!

If you decide to change the name of your award after you click on the Update Display button, just click on the mini-window and type in your changes. When you're done, click on the Update Display button again, and your new words will show up in the WordArt box.

When you've finished typing, click on the Update Display button at the bottom of the mini-window. Your words should show up in the gray box on the screen. (The gray box is called the *WordArt box.*)

5 Let's change the way the letters look by changing the typeface (the font). Click on the down arrow next to the Font box (it's the second box from the left near the top of the screen). A list of different names will drop down. To see more names, use the up and

down arrows to move through the list. Try clicking on different ones—the letters in the WordArt box will change.

6 Now let's do some neat things to your words. See the first box on the left that says *Plain Text*? That's the *Shape box*. Click on the down arrow next to the Shape box—you'll see a bunch of different shapes.

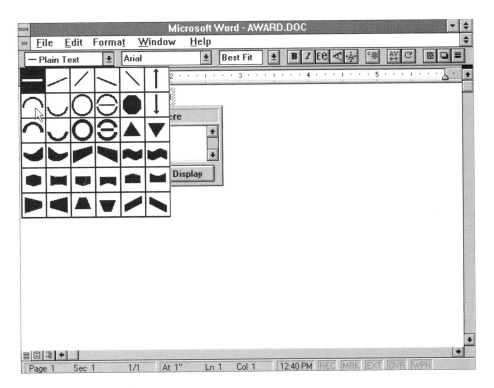

Select one of the shapes by clicking on it. The shape of your words will change to match the shape you picked! To change the shape again, just select another shape using the Shape box. (Some of the shapes, such as the ones that look like circles with lines through them, work better if you have more than one line of words typed in.)

7 Now we'll change the size of the letters to make them bigger. Click on the down arrow next to the Font Size box (it's the one to the right of the Font box). A list of numbers will

Oh No!

I Get a Message Asking If I Want to Resize the Frame!

If you see this message, just click on the Yes button.

show up. Try picking a number like 36 or 48. Just click once on a number to select it.

8 When you like the way your words look, move the pointer so it's outside the WordArt box (but not on the mini-window or the ruler).

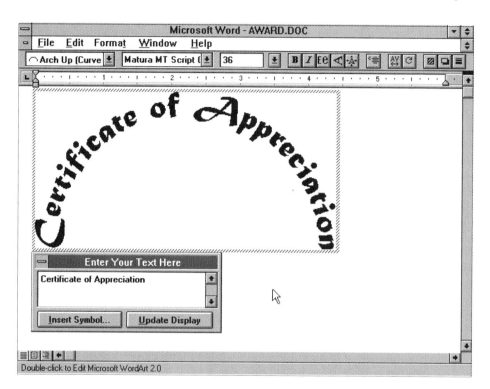

Then click on the mouse button. Now you should be back to the regular Word window, and see your award name in big, fancy letters! (If you still see the WordArt screen, make sure your pointer is in the right place, then click the mouse button again.)

9 Press the Enter or Return key to go to the next line. Then type in the rest of your award: who it's for, why it's being given, the day, who it's from—or anything else you want to add. If you want spaces between the lines, just press Enter or Return two or three times after each line you type.

If you want, change the font, the point size, and/or the style of the letters. (If you don't remember how to do this, see the Bumper Stickers project.)

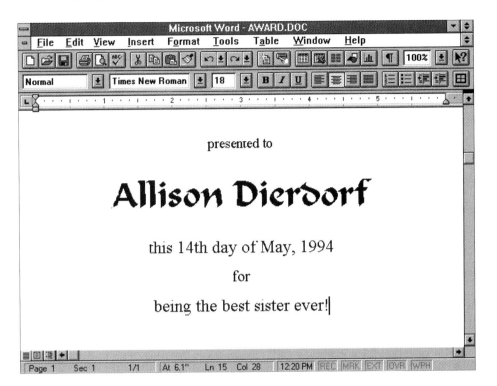

10 Most awards have centered text, so let's do that now. Select all the lines in your award (including the name of your award). Then click on the Center Alignment button, or press the Ctrl and E keys at the same time.

11 Now we'll add a fancy border around the award. Select all the lines in your award. Then go to the Format menu and select the Borders and Shading command. When the Borders and Shading dialog box appears, click on the tab at the top of the dialog box that says *Borders*. Next click on the middle white box under the word *Presets*. Then click on one of the different line styles under the word *Style* on the right side. You'll see what your border will look like in the Border box on the left side. When you've decided on the line style you like, click on the OK button.

Try This

You can make the name of the person you're giving the award to as fancy as the name of the award. Before you type in the person's name, select the Object command from the Insert menu. Then follow steps 3 through 8.

Oh No!

My Border Is Too Close to My Letters!

Here's an easy way to move the border away from the letters. Select Borders and Shading from the Format menu again, then go to the box that's next to the words *From Text*. Click on the up arrow to the right of the box to add space between your words and the border. Click on the OK button when you're done.

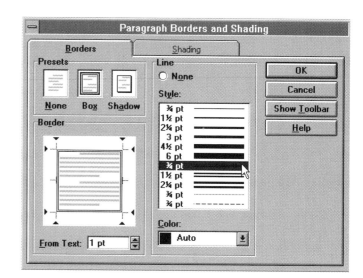

Neat Trick

To make sure your award fits on one page before you print it, choose the Print Preview command from the File menu. (see Printing Tips, page 5, for more about the Print Preview command.)

12 Save your award and print it out. (If you need to know more about saving and printing, see Saving Your Files, page 3, and Printing Tips, page 5.)

13 Now let's make a special folder for your award to keep it safe and show it off. First, fold one piece of construction paper in half across to crease it. Then, unfold the construction paper and turn it so it's tall and narrow and opens toward you. Center your certificate on the bottom half.

14 Make a pencil mark on the construction paper at each corner of the award. Then use a ruler and a pencil to draw light lines

1½ inches from each corner mark along each side of the certificate.

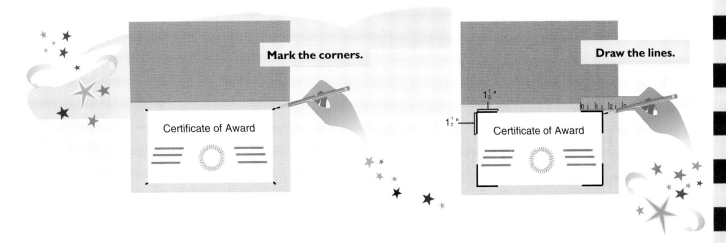

Mark the corners.

Draw the lines.

$1\frac{1}{2}"$

$1\frac{1}{2}"$

Certificate of Award

Certificate of Award

Take the award off the construction paper and connect the lines in each corner to make four small triangles. Then poke a small hole on the diagonal (the slanted line) of each triangle. Starting at the hole, carefully cut along the diagonal line of each triangle. Be careful not to cut all the way to the edges of the construction paper!

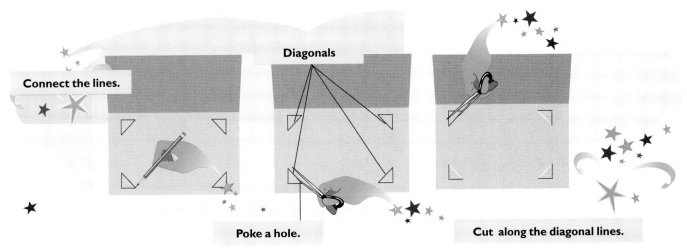

Connect the lines.

Diagonals

Poke a hole.

Cut along the diagonal lines.

15 Turn the construction paper over and put glue all over the back of it except where the slits are. Glue the second piece of construction paper to the first, making sure the edges are lined up all around.

16 When the glue is dry, fold the glued-together sheets in half across, with the slits on the inside, and crease them. Decorate the outside of the folder using markers, crayons, or even pieces of foil. To put the award in the folder, open the folder and carefully slide each corner of the award into a slit.

Try This

You can make your award certificate or folder extra fancy by adding a foil seal and ribbon. Use a ready-made seal, or make your own by cutting a small circle (1 inch to 2 inches across) out of a piece of foil wrapping or aluminum foil. Fold a small piece of ribbon in half and glue it to the back of the foil circle. Then glue the circle to the award.

Free-Flying Flags

Countries have their own flags, states have their own flags, and now you can have your own flag, too!

On the Menu

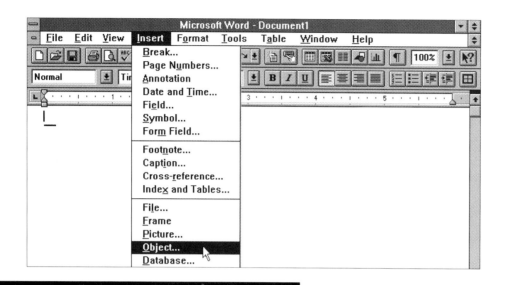

You'll Need

- *markers, crayons, or colored pencils (optional)*
- *one 8½-by-11-inch sheet of paper*
- *ruler*
- *pencil*
- *scissors*
- *dowel or cardboard coat-hanger tube or straight stick about ½ inch thick and at least 16 inches long*
- *glue stick or glue*

Continued on next page.

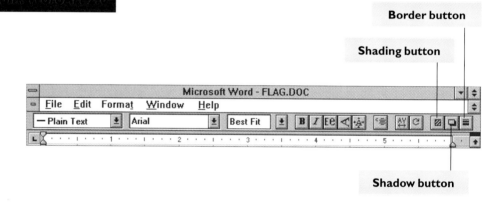

Border button

Shading button

Shadow button

Here's How to Do It

I Flags are longer than they are tall, so you first need to change your page setup to Landscape. (If you don't know how to do this, see Changing the Paper Orientation, page 2).

2 Now we'll use Word for Windows WordArt 2.0 to create a fancy design for your flag. To get to WordArt, go to the Insert menu and select the Object command. When the Object dialog box appears, click on the tab at the top of the box that says *Create New*. Then click on the

name *Microsoft WordArt 2.0* from the list of names. Next click on the OK button.

3 Find the mini-window that says *Enter Your Text Here*. Type in your name. (When you start typing, the words in the mini-window will be erased.) When you've finished typing, click on the Update Display button at the bottom of the mini-window. Your name should show up in the gray WordArt box on the screen.

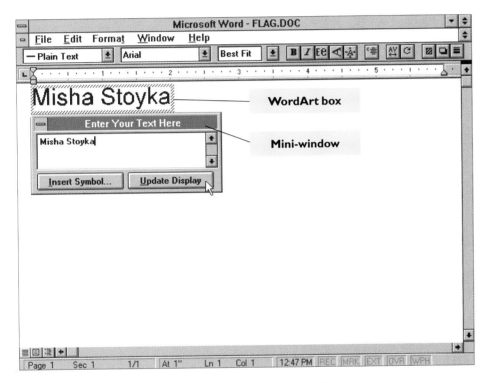

4 Play around with the way your name looks by using the Shape and Font boxes in the upper-left hand side. (If you need more help with how to use these boxes, see steps 5 and 6 of the Amazing Awards project.)

5 Now let's make your name look really cool. See the three buttons on the right-hand side above the ruler? These are the *Shading button*, the *Shadow button*, and the *Border button*. First try clicking on the Shading button (it's the one with the slanted lines inside the box). The Shading dialog box appears.

You'll Need

(continued)

• **WordArt 2.0 (this program comes with Word for Windows; if WordArt 2.0 is not present, ask a grown-up to use the Word for Windows disks to install it)**

Oh No!

I Get a Message Asking If I Want to Resize the Frame!

If you see this message, just click on the Yes button.

Neat Trick

You can test out how your name will look by using the Apply button. Just click on a pattern, then click on the Apply button. Your name will fill with the pattern, but the Shading dialog box won't disappear. (If you need to move the box to see your name, just move the pointer to the top of the dialog box, then hold down the mouse button and drag the dialog box out of the way.) When you find the pattern you want to use, click on the OK button.

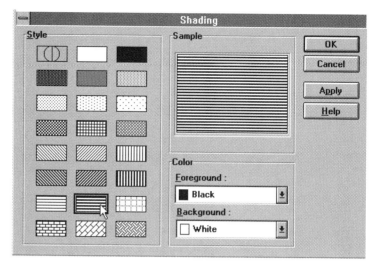

The Shading dialog box

Pick one of the patterns in the Style box by clicking on it. Then click on the OK button. Each letter in your name will be filled with the pattern!

6 Now let's add a border around each letter. Click on the Border button (the one with the three lines on it). Then, when the Border dialog box shows up, click on one of the lines in the Thickness box.

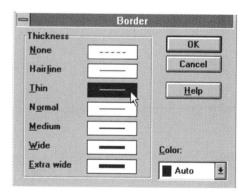

Click on the OK button, and you will see a line around each letter.

7 You can also add a shadow to your name. Click once on the Shadow button—it's between the Border and Shading buttons. You'll see eight different kinds of shadows. Try clicking on one to see what happens!

8 Use the Shading, Border, and Shadow buttons until you like the way your name looks. Then move the pointer (the arrow) so it's outside the gray WordArt box (but not on the mini-window or ruler), and click the mouse button once. You'll be back to the regular Word window, and the first part of your flag will be done.

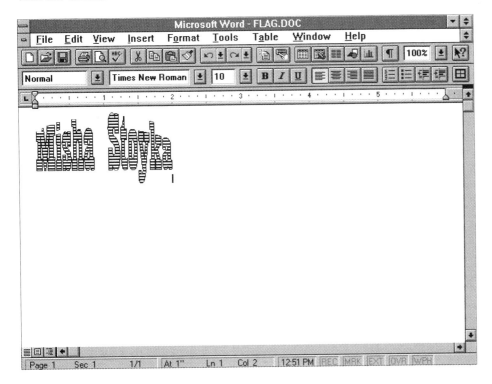

9 Now we'll make your flag even fancier. First, select your name—just click on it once. You'll see a black box appear around your name. Next, select the Copy command from the Edit menu. Move the pointer so it's outside the box around your name, and click the mouse button—the box will disappear. Then go back to the Edit menu and choose the Paste command. A second copy of your name appears!

10 Use the mouse to double-click on the second copy of your name. The WordArt window shows up again. Use the different

Try This

You can change how the patterns look by changing the foreground color and background color in the Shading dialog box. Click on the down arrow next to the Foreground Color box or Background Color box, and select one of the colors that shows up by clicking on it. You'll see what the pattern looks like in the Sample box. Play around until you like the way the pattern looks, then click on the OK button. (But remember, you can't print out the colors unless you have a color printer.)

Try This

WordArt lets you do a lot of fancy things to your letters and words. Here's something else you might want to try. You can make your letters turn on their side by clicking the Flip button (it's the one that looks like a sideways *A*). Click the Flip button a second time, and your letters will be back to normal.

Oh No!

My Flag Prints Out on More Than One Page!

If your flag prints out on more than one page, you can make the size of the type smaller (use the Size box in the WordArt window), change the top or bottom margins (see the Dandy Doorknob Hangers project for more on changing margins), or remove some of the names you copied and changed. To get rid of extra names, select the name, and press the Backspace or Delete key.

Try This

If you want a design on both sides of your flag, you can print out two copies of the flag, and glue one to each side of the paper flap. Make sure the flag edges are lined up and the printed sides are facing out. Then glue the backs of the flags together so they don't flop apart.

buttons to change the way your name looks. Then click outside the gray WordArt box to return to the regular Word window.

11 Try repeating steps 9 and 10 a few more times, until your name appears in many different styles. If you want to put your name on different lines, just press the Enter or Return key before you use the Paste command. Or, if you want spaces between the name boxes, just press the Spacebar a few times before you paste. Remember, if you don't like the way one of your name boxes looks, double-click on it to get back to the WordArt window. Then change the way it looks, and click outside the WordArt box to get back to Word.

12 When you like your flag, save it and print it out. (For more on saving and printing, see Saving Your Files, page 3, and Printing Tips, page 5.) Color your flag, if you wish.

13 Now you're ready to put the flag on a flagpole. Use your ruler to draw a straight line across a blank piece of paper. The line should be about 4 inches from the top. Cut along the line. Then, fold the smaller piece of paper in half lengthwise. Open it and put glue on one side of the paper.

14 Lay the dowel or other stick along the fold, lining up the end of the dowel with the top edge of the paper. Hold the paper against the dowel at the fold and line it up so the two sides are even. Press the sides together to make a flap. Then, smooth the paper tightly around the dowel so there's no space where the two sides of the paper meet.

4"

Cut a strip.

Fold in half lengthwise.

Add glue.

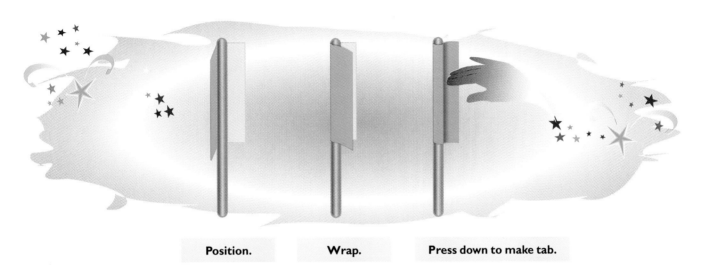

Position.

Wrap.

Press down to make tab.

15 Put glue on one side of the paper flap and glue it to the back of your flag along one edge. When the glue is dry, your flag is ready to fly!

Glue flag to flap.

Video Game Collector Cards

How many video games do you have? With these collector cards you can keep track of your games and share your playing tips at the same time!

Yoshi's Cookie

Machine Type		Players
Nintendo		1 or 2
Theme		Levels
Action		100
Special Stuff		
Has an extra puzzle game and bonus rounds		

TIPS

You can reach higher levels usi...
this trick. Go to the Option...
Set the music to Off and...
to High. Choose R...
hold Up on yo...
press Select...
to Round 1...
round, press S...
Right on your con...

Jurassic Park

Machine Type		Players
Sega Genesis		1
Theme		Levels
Action		7
Special Stuff		
Can choose to be Grant or the Raptor		

TIPS

...rest caverns,
...and on the
...st other
...em with
...he bottom of
...to stay back.
...ledge and
...the B button

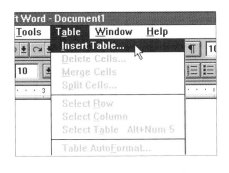
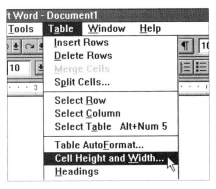
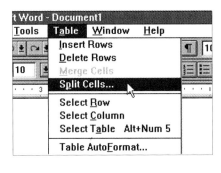

Here's How to Do It

I Collector cards usually have lots of information on them. We're going to use Word for Windows tables to create boxes for the information. First, go to the Table menu and select the Insert Table command. You'll see the Insert Table dialog box, like this:

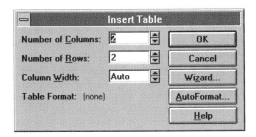

You probably know what columns and rows are, but just in case you don't, columns are up and down (vertical) sections, and rows are left to right (horizontal) sections. We want to start by making a table with one column and five rows. To do this, select the number in the Number of Columns box, and type the number **1**. Next, select the number in the Number of Rows box and type the number **5**. Click on the OK button. Your boxes should show up on the screen. (If you don't see any lines on your screen, go back to

You'll Need

- **3-by-5-inch white index cards (one for each collector card)**
- **markers, crayons, or colored pencils, or game illustrations from ads, magazines, or packages**
- **glue stick or glue**
- **scissors**
- **ruler**
- **pencil**
- **clear contact paper**

the Table menu and select the last command—Gridlines. The lines should show up.)

2 Next, we need to make the column smaller, so the table will fit on an index card. To do this, select the table. Then go to the Table menu and select the Cell Height and Width command. When the dialog box appears, click on the tab that says *Column*. Then select the number in the box next to the words *Width of Column 1* and type the number **3**. Click on the OK button. You'll see the table is narrower!

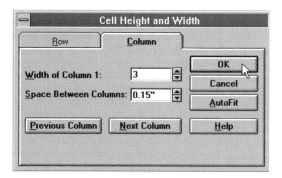

3 Now, let's make two boxes (called *cells*) instead of one in some of the rows. Move your mouse so the pointer is at the very left edge of the second row. The pointer should change into an arrow. Select both row 2 and row 3 by holding down the mouse button and dragging the mouse.

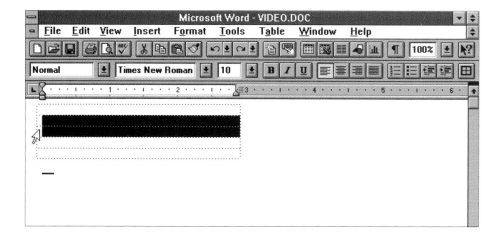

4 Go to the Table menu and select the Split Cells command. The Split Cells dialog box will appear.

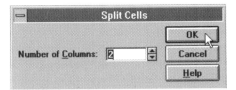

Make sure you see the number 2 in the Number of Columns box. (If you don't, select the number in the box, then type in a **2**.) Then click on the OK button. Now the second and third rows have two cells each!

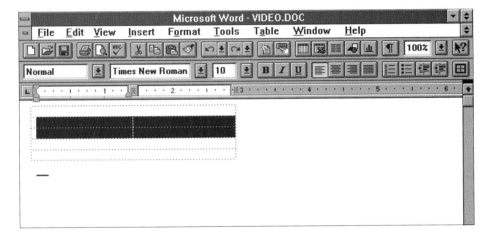

5 Now you can type in information about your video game. Type in the name of the game in the first row. Then press the Tab key to move to the next cell. In the cells in the second row, you might want to type in the type of machine you play on and the number of players. In the cells in the third row, you might want to tell what the theme of the game is and how many levels it has. Use the fourth row to tell about characters in the game or special features such as bonus rounds. And in the fifth row, try adding tricks and tips you can use in the game. If you want more space between the rows, just press the Enter or Return key after a line.

Oh No!

I Split the Wrong Cells!

To put the cells back together again, just select the cells, then choose the Merge Cells command from the Table menu. That's it!

Neat Trick

You can use the Tab key to move from cell to cell in the table. Or, you can use the mouse—just move the pointer into a cell and click the mouse button.

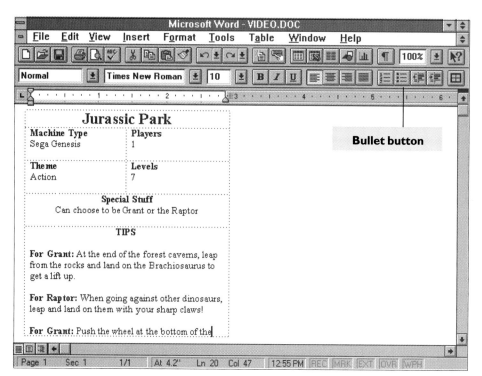

The filled in table

Neat Trick

If you want little dots (called bullets) before each tip, go to the button that has three little squares on it (it's four in from the right). Click on the button and a bullet appears. Now type in your tip. When you press the Enter or Return key to go to the next line, Word will put in the next bullet for you. To stop adding bullets, just click on the Bullet button again.

6 If you want, change the typeface (the font), the size of the letters (the point size), and the alignment. (If you don't know how to do these things, see the Bumper Stickers and Party Placemats projects.)

7 Next, we need to put lines that print around the cells. (The ones you see on the screen now won't print out.) Select all the cells in the table. Then go to the Format menu and select the Borders and Shading command. A Borders and Shading dialog box will appear. Click on the Borders tab.

8 Click on the middle white box under the word *Presets*. You'll see what your border will look like in the Border box on the left side. Because we want lines around all the cells, you need to click the pointer in the middle of the lines of the Border box, like this:

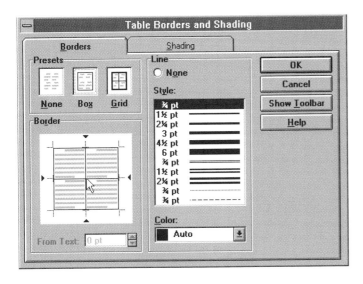

When you've created the border, click on the OK button. You'll see there are lines all around your cells!

9 Let's check to make sure your card is less than five inches long. You can do this by clicking the mouse pointer at the end of the last line of your card. Then look at the gray bar at the bottom of the window. See the different words and numbers? Find the number just after the word *At*. If the number is over 5, you have to delete some lines in your card. If the number is under 5, you're fine.

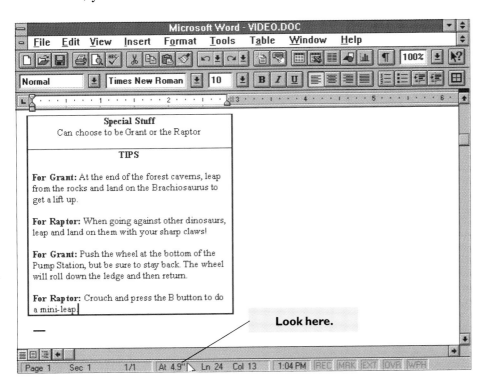

Try This

Try making other kinds of collector cards: book collector cards, baseball collector cards, movie star collector cards—whatever you can think of!

10 Save your card and print it out. Decorate one side of the index card with drawings, or cut out pictures of the game from magazines, ads, or even the game box and glue them on the index card.

11 Next, cut out the card you printed along the outside lines. Put glue on the back of the printed piece, and paste it onto the blank side of the index card. Make sure the left and right edges are lined up with the edges of the index card. Let the glue dry.

12 Now we'll make the card waterproof. Use a ruler and a pencil to draw two 3¼-by-5¼-inch boxes on the contact paper. Cut out the pieces. Peel the backing off one of the pieces and put it, sticky-side up, on a hard surface. Position your collector card so it's centered on the contact paper.

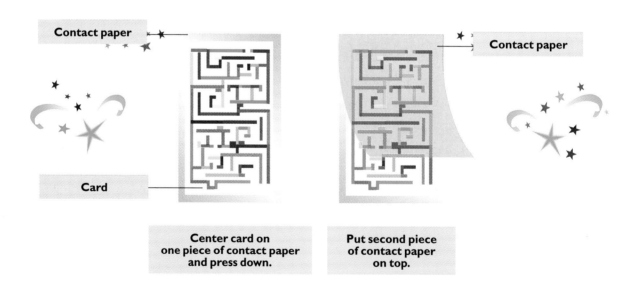

Contact paper

Card

Center card on one piece of contact paper and press down.

Contact paper

Put second piece of contact paper on top.

13 Peel the backing off the other piece of contact paper. Line it up over the card so its edges match the edges of the bottom piece of contact paper. Lower it down, and smooth it with your hands. Now it's ready to show off!

Wacky Wall Calendars

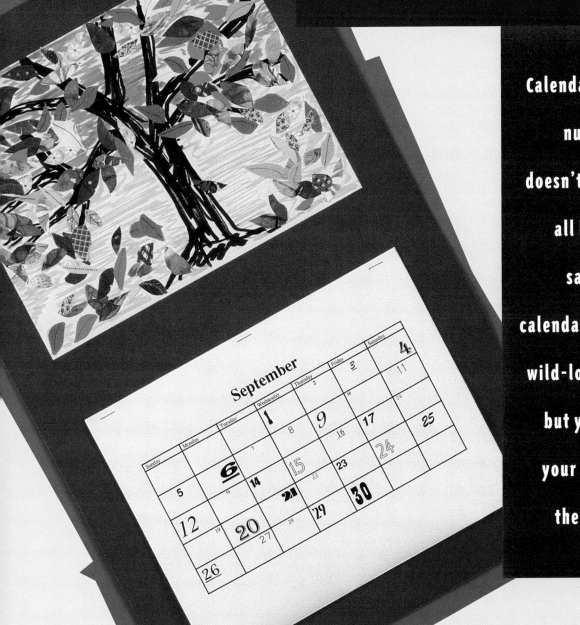

Calendars may all have numbers, but that doesn't mean that they all have to look the same. These crazy calendars not only have wild-looking numbers, but you can also add your own art to make them extra special.

On the Menu

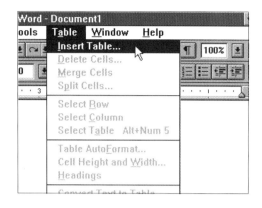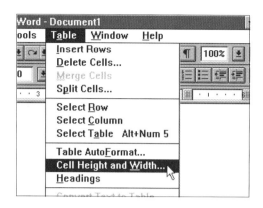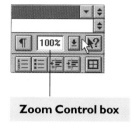

Zoom Control box

You'll Need

- **three or more 8½-by-11-inch pieces of printer paper**
- **stapler**
- **one 14-by-22-inch piece of poster board, any color**
- **pencil**
- **glue stick or glue**
- **markers, crayons, or colored pencils (optional)**
- **scissors (optional)**
- **colored paper, magazine pictures, and/or photos (optional)**

Here's How to Do It

1 First you need to change your page setup to Landscape, so your page will be wider than it is long. (If you don't know how to do this, see Changing the Paper Orientation, page 2.)

2 We'll start by making a one-month calendar. First decide what month your calendar is going to show. Then type in the name of the month, and press the Enter or Return key twice.

3 Most calendars have one box for each day of the month. We can use Word for Windows tables to make all the boxes at once. Just go to the Table menu and select the Insert Table command. You'll need seven columns—one for each day of the week—so in the Number of Columns box, type the number 7. Then, in the Number of Rows box, type the number **6** or **7** (five or six rows for each possible week in a

month, plus an extra row to write in the days
of the week).

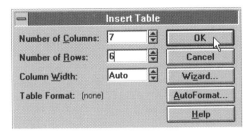

Click on the OK button when you're done. If you
don't see any lines on your screen, go back to
the Table menu and select the last command—
Gridlines. The lines should show up.

4 Now let's type in the days of the week. Most
calendars start with Sunday as the first day,
so type in **Sunday**. Press the Tab key to go to the
next box (or *cell*) on the right. Then type in the
next day of the week—**Monday**—and press the
Tab key again. Keep doing this until you've
typed in all the days of the week.

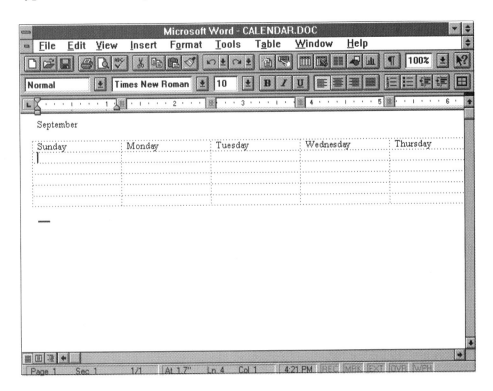

5 You probably noticed that you can't see all of your calendar at one time. To change this, you can use the Zoom Control box (it's the box that says *100%* in the top row of buttons). Just click on the down arrow next to the box, and you'll see a list of numbers and words. Click on the words *Page Width*.

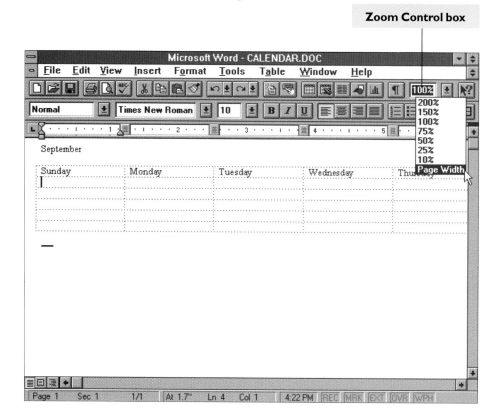

Zoom Control box

You'll now see the whole calendar on the screen! If you want to go back to normal, click the Zoom Control button again, and then click on 100% in the list.

6 Now type in the number for each day of the month. Just click in a cell, type in the number, and then hit the Tab key to go to the next cell. Remember, the first day of the month doesn't always start on a Sunday. Check another calendar to see which is the first day of the month you picked.

Oh No!

I Made Only 6 Rows, but I Need 7!

Don't worry if you don't have enough rows—it's easy to add another. Just use the Tab key to go to the last cell in your table. Then press the Tab key again. Ta da! You now have another row!

7 Next, let's make all the number boxes bigger, so you'll have room to write in important messages and reminders. Go to the first cell in the second row (even if it's empty) and select all the cells below it in the column (even the empty ones).

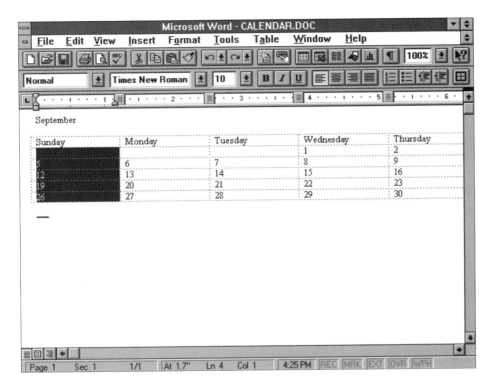

Oh No!

I Made 7 Rows, but I Need Only 6!

To get rid of an extra row that you don't need, click the mouse pointer in one of the cells in the row you don't want. Then go to the Table menu and select the Select Row command. Next, go back to the Table menu and select the Delete Rows command. Now your extra row is gone!

8 Next select the Cell Height and Width command from the Table menu. When the dialog box appears, click on the tab that says *Row*. Then click on the down arrow next to the box under the words *Height of Rows 2-7 (or 6)*. Pick the last choice, *Exactly*. This means that all your boxes will be the same size.

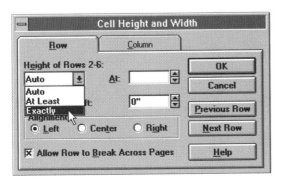

Now you have to pick the size of the cells. Go to the box next to the word *At* and type in **5 li** (the *li* stands for lines). Click on the OK button when you're done. Now your table will have much bigger boxes.

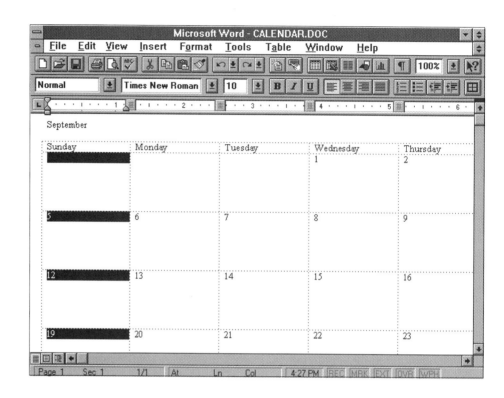

9 Let's add some lines around the cells in the table. Select all the cells in the table. Then use the Borders and Shading command from the Format menu to add a border around all the cells. (If you need help with this, see steps 6 and 7 of the Video Game Collector Cards project.)

10 Now that you have a basic calendar, let's jazz it up some. Select one of the numbers. Then change the typeface (the font), the size of the number (the point size), the alignment, and whether the number is bold, italic, or underlined (the style). (If you need to know how to do these things, see the Bumper Stickers and Party Placemats projects.) Try doing something different for every number of the month!

11 Now go back and select the name of the month you typed in. Press the Ctrl key and E together to center the name. Try changing the font or point size to make the month name stand out.

12 When you like how your calendar looks, save it and print it out. (If you need help with saving and printing, see Saving Your Files, page 3 and Printing Tips, page 5.) If you want, make calendars for other months in the year, too.

13 Put your printed calendar sheet on top of one of the blank sheets of paper. Make sure the edges match all around, then staple the two pieces together at the top. (Use three staples— one at each side and one in the middle.)

14 Turn the poster board so it's tall and narrow. Center the stapled sheets on the bottom half of the poster board so there's about the same amount of board showing at the bottom and at each side. When you're sure the calendar is centered, make a light mark with a pencil on the poster board at each corner of your calendar.

Neat Trick

If you want to have two or more numbers look the same, you can use special Copy and Paste commands, called Copy Format and Paste Format. First, select a number you like the look of, then press three keys at the same time—the Ctrl key, the Shift key, and C. Next, select the second number that you want to look the same as the first. Now press another set of three keys—the Ctrl key, the Shift key, and V.

Center the calendar.

Mark position.

Glue in place.

Put glue on the back of the blank sheet that's stapled to the calendar and glue it to the poster board. Make sure you match up each corner with one of the pencil marks, and that the bottom of the calendar is near the bottom of the poster board. Press the glued sheet onto the poster board and smooth out the wrinkles.

15 If you want, make a picture for your wall calendar on a piece of plain paper. Anything goes. You can pick a subject that matches your calendar month. You can be silly or serious. You can draw a design or cartoon, or glue on cut-out magazine pictures. When you have a picture you like, staple it to a blank sheet, just as you did with the calendar sheet in step 13.

16 Center the picture on the top half of the poster board. Leave about the same amount of poster board showing all the way around. Make a pencil mark at each corner, then glue down the picture as you did for the calendar in step 14.

Center and mark art.

Glue down

Add a thumbtack or pushpin, and your calendar is ready to hang! If you have more than one page in your calendar, just tear off each calendar sheet at the end of the month.

Fantastic Flip Books

Make your own "movie" of a van that runs back and forth. What's the secret? You use Word for Windows tables to make a set of pictures, each with the van in a slightly different place. Then you make the pictures into a book. Flip quickly through the book and see the van move!

On the Menu

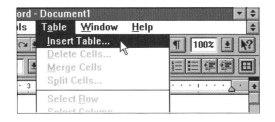 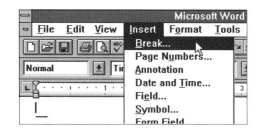 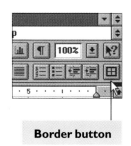

Border button

You'll Need

- **scissors**
- **at least ten 3-by-5-inch index cards (white or colored)**
- **newspaper**
- **glue stick or glue**
- **2 rubber bands**
- **cloth or plastic tape at least 1¼" wide (optional)**
- **markers, crayons, or colored pencils (optional)**

Here's How to Do It

Flip books are pretty small, so you need to change the page margins to make the flip book the right size. This is easy to do—just go to the File menu and select the Page Setup command. When the Page Setup dialog box appears, click on the Margins tab. Then go to the box next to the word *Right*. Select the number in the box and press the Backspace or Delete key—the number is erased. Now type **4.75** in the box. After you type in the number, click on the OK button.

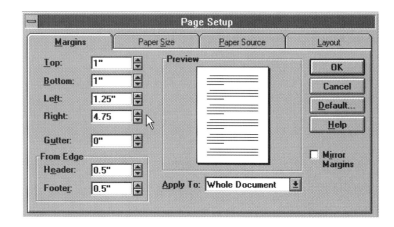

2 Now you need to make a table. Go to the Table menu and select the Insert Table command. You'll need a table that has ten columns and eight rows, so type in **10** in the Number of Columns box and **8** in the Number of Rows box. Then click the OK button. (If you don't see any lines on your screen, go back to the Table menu and select the last command— Gridlines. The lines should show up.)

3 Next we need to put a border around the table. Select the whole table (you can do this quickly by selecting the Select Table command from the Table menu). Then choose the Borders and Shading command from the Format menu. When the dialog box appears, click on the Borders tab, then click on the middle white box under the word *Presets*. After you do that, click on the second line in the list under the word *Style*. Then, click on the OK button when you're done.

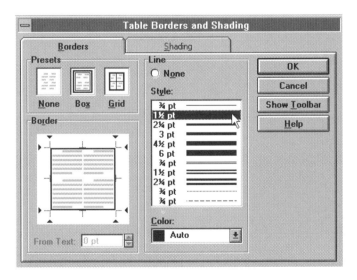

4 We're almost ready to start making the van, but first we need to do one more thing— make copies of the table. Luckily, the Copy and

Paste commands make this easy. Make sure your table is still selected. Then go to the Edit menu and select Copy (or press the Ctrl key and C at the same time). Next, click the mouse below the table. Press the Enter or Return key once. Then go back to the Edit menu and select the Paste command (or press the Ctrl key and V at the same time). You'll see two tables.

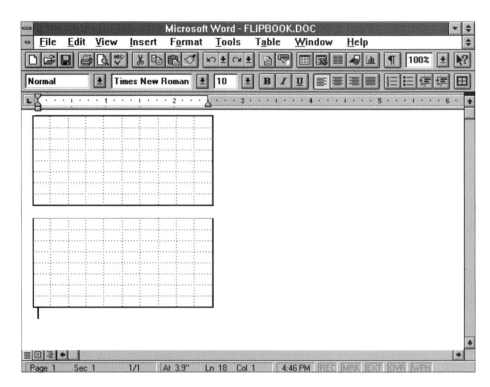

5 Do this three more times, so you have five tables. Now, let's make sure the end of the page doesn't break up a table. The blinking line (the *insertion point*) should be flashing beneath the bottom of the fifth table. Then pull down the Insert menu and select the Break command— it's the first one. You'll see the Break dialog box.

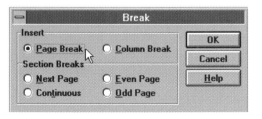

See if there's a black dot in the circle next to the words *Page Break*. If there isn't, click on the circle so the black dot appears. Then press the OK button. You'll see a gray line with the word *Page Break* in the middle. This tells you where the page ends, but it doesn't show up when you print out the page.

6 Copy and paste your table four more times, so you have a total of nine tables.

7 Now we'll start on the van. Go back to the very first table you made. Use the mouse to select the two left-hand boxes (cells) in the third row from the bottom. Then click on the Border button (it's the one with four small squares on the right side). Some new buttons and boxes will show up.

Neat Trick

You can select the first four tables you made, and copy and paste them all at once.

Oh No!

I Made Too Many Tables!

If you make an extra table by accident, select the extra table. Then go to the Edit menu and select the Cut command. The extra table will disappear!

Shading box · · · Border button

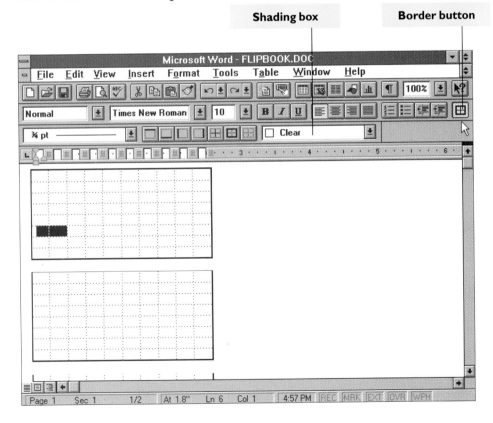

Find the box that says *Clear*—this box is the Shading box. Click on the down arrow to the right of the Shading box, then click on 50%

shading. The pattern will appear in the cells you selected.

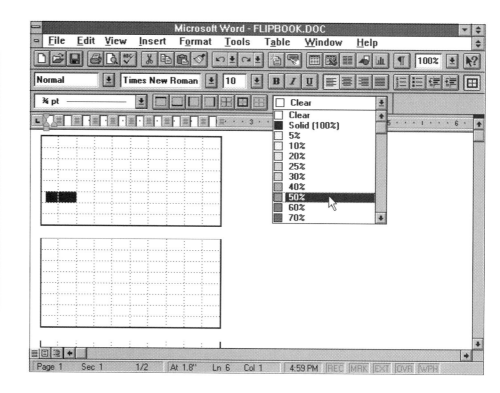

Oh No!

I Put Shading in the Wrong Boxes!

Don't worry—just select the cells that shouldn't have shading in them. Click on the arrow next to the Shading box again, then click on the choice that says *Clear*.

8 Use the Tab key or down arrow key to move to the cell just below the first shaded cell. Type in a capital letter **O**. Move to the next cell on the right and type in another capital **O**. Now you have your van!

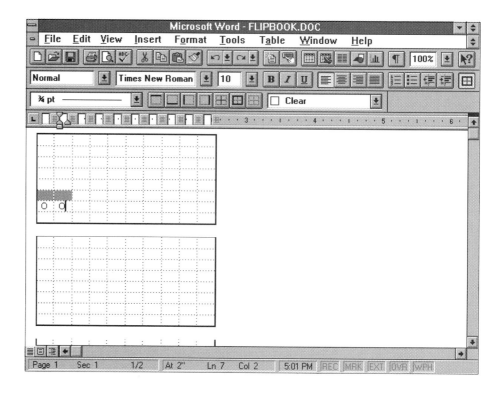

9 Now let's make a van in the next table. Go to the third row from the bottom of the second table. This time, instead of selecting the first two cells on the left, select the second and third cells. Then repeat steps 7 and 8 to make a second van.

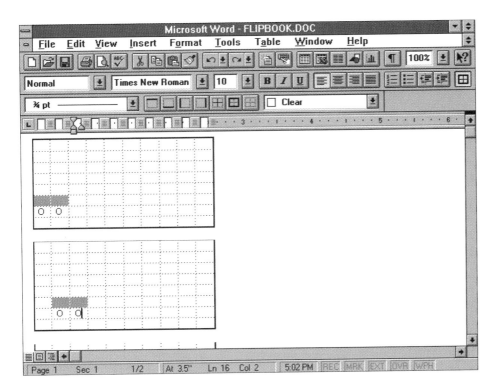

10 Go to the third table, and move to the third cell in the third row from the bottom. Make the van again. Keep making a van in each table, moving the van over one cell to the right each time, until the van is in the two right-hand cells in table 9.

11 Save your tables and print them out. You need at least two copies of your tables. (If you need help with saving and printing, see Saving Your Files, page 3, and Printing Tips, page 5.) Next, cut out each boxed table. You may want to write a tiny number in the upper left-hand corner of each table, so you can keep them in order after they've been cut out.

12 Next, let's put together the flip book. Fold each index card in half across. Cut along the folds.

13 Now you're going to glue each table to an index card half. It's easier to do this in groups. Lay out nine index-card halves on the newspaper. Lay nine cut-out tables face down on some clean paper and put glue on the back of each one. Put each table on a card, lining up the bottom edge of the table with the bottom edge of the card. The tables should fit exactly across the cards.

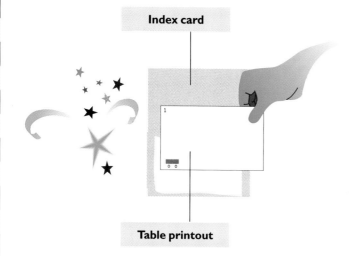

Index card

Table printout

Repeat until all the tables are glued onto the cards. You'll have two card halves left over that will be your front and back covers.

14 Stack the cards with the tables facing up in order from 1 to 9 and then from 9 to 1. Put one of the blank cards on the top of the stack and the other on the bottom of the stack. Then glue the cards together at the end opposite from the tables. Start by putting a 1-inch strip of glue along the top edge of the bottom card (the back cover) and put the next card face up on top of it, lining them up at the edges.

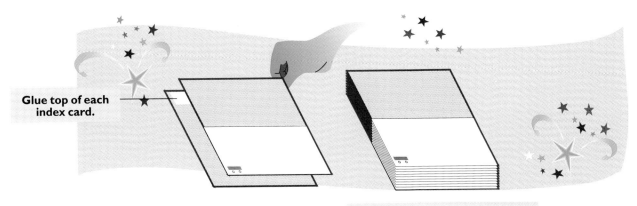

Glue top of each index card.

The stack of cards, after gluing.

Repeat until all the cards are glued. Try to keep the edges as even as possible. Then put two rubber bands tightly around the cards, one in each direction. This will hold the book together while it dries.

Rubber bands

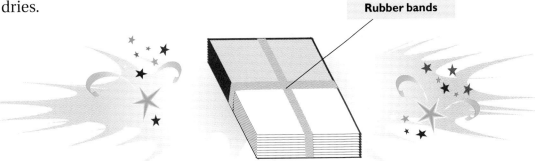

15 When the book is dry, put a piece of tape or glue a piece of paper over the glued end to cover it. Decorate the cover as you wish. (You might try printing an extra copy of a table so you can cut out a picture of the van for a cover illustration.) To watch your movie, hold the glued end of the book with one hand, and use the thumb of your other hand to flip quickly through the pages.

Try This

Here are some other objects you might use instead of the van in your flip book. (The squares are just to show you where the cells are.) Or just experiment to see what you can come up with!

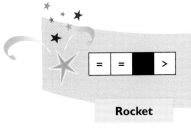

Rocket

Train

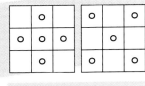

Spinning wheel— alternate between these two pictures.

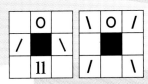

Jumping person— alternate between these two pictures.

Pen and Pencil Holders

You don't have to keep these colorful pen and pencil holders for yourself. Make some as presents for your friends and family, too!

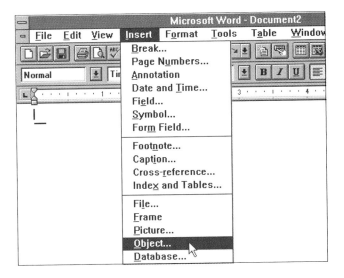

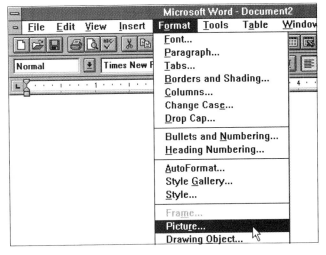

Additional Program: Microsoft Picture

Line Tool

Ellipse Tool

Selection Tool

Rectangle Tool

Arc Tool

Page 1 Sec 1 1/1 At 4.5" Ln 1 Col

Close Picture

Close Picture button

You'll Need

- *markers, crayons, or colored pencils*
- *scissors*
- *glue stick or glue*
- *empty 12-ounce frozen juice can*
- *ruler*
- *pencil*
- *clear contact paper*
- *Microsoft Picture (This program comes with Word for Windows. If it is not present, ask a grown-up to use the Word for Windows disks to install it.)*

Here's How to Do It

The first thing you need to do is change your page setup to Landscape. (If you don't know how to do this, see Changing the Paper Orientation, page 2.)

2 Now we'll start on the holder. We're going to use a special feature called Microsoft Picture that lets you draw pictures in Word. To use this feature, go to the Insert menu and select the Object command—it's the second-to-last one in the list. The Object dialog box will appear on the screen.

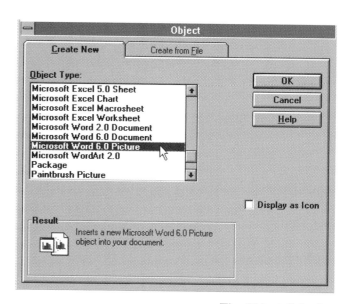

The Object dialog box

Click on the tab with the words *Create New* at the top of the dialog box. Then find the name *Microsoft Word 6.0 Picture* in the list and click on it. (If you need to, use the up and down arrows to find the name.) Now click on the OK button. You should see a window with a gray box in the middle of it (called the Boundary box). This is where you draw your picture.

Boundary box

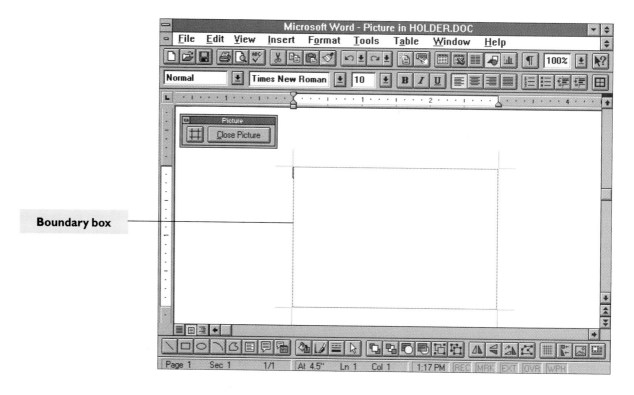

3 Let's start by drawing a rectangle. At the bottom of the screen, you'll see a bunch of different buttons. Find the button with the rectangle on it—that's the Rectangle Tool button. Click on the button to select it.

Move the pointer over to the white space in the window. The pointer will change to a plus sign (+). Then move the pointer to the upper-left corner of the Boundary box so the middle of the plus sign is right near the corner. Hold down the mouse button and drag the pointer to the lower-right corner of the white space. You'll see the lines of your rectangle on the screen.

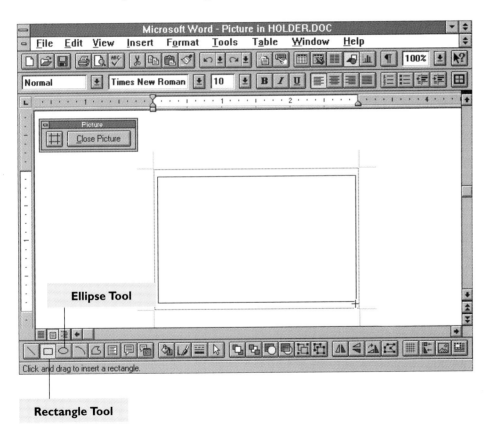

The size of the rectangle will change as you move the pointer. When the rectangle is the right size, let go of the mouse button.

Now let's draw an oval inside the rectangle. Click on the button at the bottom of your screen with the oval on it (called the Ellipse Tool button). Then move the pointer back to the white space, inside the rectangle. Hold down the mouse button and drag the mouse. An oval will appear on the screen! Keep the mouse button down and move the mouse around—you'll see that the oval changes shape. When you see the shape you like, let go of the mouse button.

It's easy to change the shape or size of something after you've drawn it. First, find and click on the button at the bottom of your screen with the arrow on it (it's called the Selection Tool button). Then click on the shape you don't like. Some tiny squares (called handles) will appear around the shape.

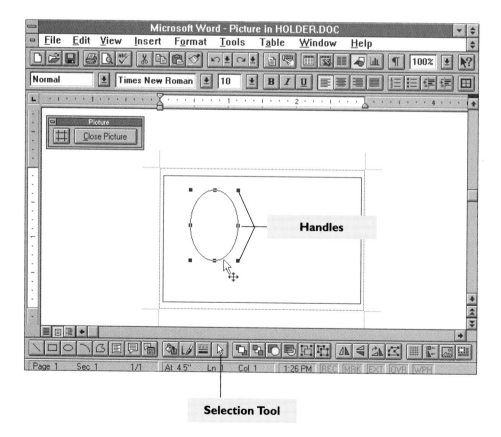

Put the pointer over one of the handles, hold down the mouse button, and drag the mouse. The way your shape looks will change as you move the mouse. When you get your shape the way you want it, let go of the mouse button.

6 You can also move shapes around after you draw them. To move the oval, click on the Selection Tool button, then move the arrow so it's over your oval. Hold down the mouse button, then drag. You'll see a second oval with dotted lines that moves as you move your mouse. When the second oval is where you want it, let go of the mouse button. The second oval disappears, and your original oval is in the new place!

7 Try using the other shape tools to make different shapes inside the first rectangle you drew. To draw arcs, click on the Arc Tool button (it's the one with the curved line on it). To draw a line, click on the Line Tool button (it has the slanted line on it). Then use the mouse as you did in steps 3 through 6. Move the shapes around, and change their sizes until you have a picture or pattern that you like.

8 When you're finished with your picture, find the tiny window that holds the Close Picture button. It looks like this:

Click on the button. The Microsoft Picture window will close and you'll see your drawing in your Word window!

9 Now we'll make your picture just the right size for a pen and pencil holder. Click on the picture to select it (you'll see a line with several

Oh No!

I Want to Get Rid of a Shape!

If you want to get rid of a shape and start again, click once on the shape with the Selection Tool to select it. Then press the Delete key. Your shape will disappear.

Neat Trick

To make perfect squares or circles, hold down the Shift key when you drag the mouse. That's all there is to it! (You can use this trick to make straight lines, too—just hold down the Shift key when you use the Line Tool.)

Oh No!

I Want to Change My Picture!

If you want to make changes after you've clicked on the Close Picture button, just double-click on your picture. The Microsoft Picture window will open back up again.

tiny black boxes around the edges of your picture). Then go to the Format menu and select the Picture command (it's the second-to-last one on the list). You will see the Picture dialog box.

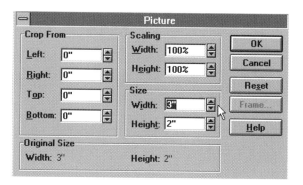

See the Size box? Inside the Size box are two white boxes—the Width box and the Height box. Select the number in the Width box and use the Backspace or Delete key to erase the number. Then type in the numbers **8.5**. Then click in the Height box. Erase the numbers, and type in **4.7**.

10 Click on the OK button when you're done. Your picture is now much bigger! Save your picture and print it out. (If you need help doing this see Saving Your Files, page 3, and Printing Tips, page 5.)

11 Now it's time to put your pen and pencil holder together. Use markers, crayons, or colored pencils to color and decorate your picture. Then cut out the picture along the edges of the outside box.

12 Next, use a ruler and a pencil to draw a 8½-by-4¾-inch rectangle on the contact paper. Peel off the backing, and place the contact paper on a hard surface with the sticky side up. Hold your cut-out picture face down over the contact paper, lining up the left and right edges. Slowly lower it onto the contact paper, smoothing as you go. Trim off any contact paper that sticks out from the edges of the picture.

13 Put glue on the back of your picture, then wrap the picture the long way around the juice can; smooth out any wrinkles. Make sure the edges line up at the top and bottom rims of the can. Let it dry. Collect some pens and pencils and show off your holder.

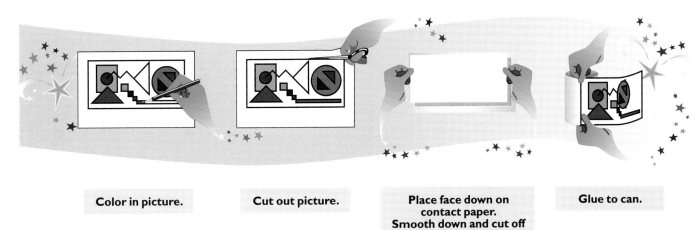

Color in picture.

Cut out picture.

Place face down on contact paper. Smooth down and cut off any extra contact paper.

Glue to can.

Mini Pocket Folders

You've probably used pocket folders to hold papers for school. But did you know you could use Word for Windows to make your own? These mini pocket folders are great for carrying notes, to-do lists, coupons, even photographs

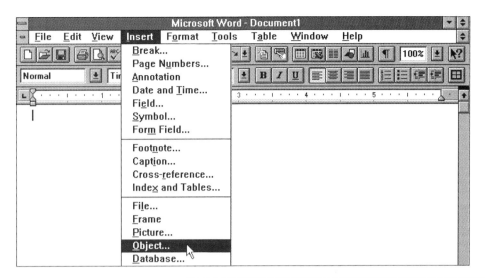

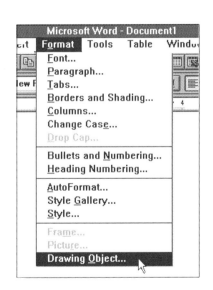

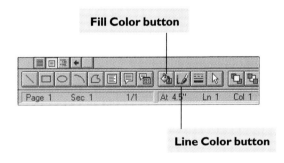

Fill Color button

Line Color button

You'll Need

- *markers, crayons, or colored pencils*
- *glitter glue stick or glitter (optional)*
- *pencil*
- *ruler*
- *glue stick or glue*
- *Microsoft Picture (This program comes with Word for Windows. If Microsoft Picture is not present, ask a grown-up to use the Word for Windows disks to install it.)*

Here's How to Do It

We're going to make the folders from one sheet of paper, so we need to change the page around a bit to do this. First, change your page setup to Landscape. (If you need help doing this, see Changing the Paper Orientation, page 2.) Then select the Page Setup command from the File menu. Click on the tab that says *Margins*. Then type **1** in the box next to the word *Top*. Type **2** in the box next to the word *Bottom*. Type **6** in the box next to the word *Left*. And type **1** in the box next to the word *Right*. Now click on the OK button.

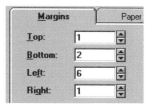

2 Now we're going to use Microsoft Picture to create a fancy picture for your folder. To get to Picture, go to the Insert menu and select the Object command. Click on the Create New tab. Then select *Microsoft Word 6.0 Picture* from the list of names in the Object dialog box, and click on the OK button.

3 Use the Line and Shape tools to make lines and shapes within the Boundary box (the gray lines) in the Picture window. (If you don't know how to do this, see steps 3 through 7 of the Pen and Pencil Holders project).

4 If you want, you can change the way your lines look, or make them thicker or thinner. Click on the Selection Tool button (it's the one with the arrow on it). Use the Selection Tool to select a line. Go to the Format menu and select the Drawing Object command. When the Drawing Object dialog box appears, click on the Line tab, You'll see the Line Style dialog box.

Use the Style box choices to change the type of line you have. Use the Color box choices to change the color of your line. Use the Weight

Neat Trick

You can copy and paste the shapes and lines you make, just like you copy and paste words. To copy, use the Selection Tool (the one that looks like an arrow) to select a shape or line. (If you want to copy several shapes and lines at one time, hold down the Shift key and click on each object.) Then go to the Edit menu and select the Copy command. Pull down the Edit menu again, and pick the Paste command—a copy of your shape or line will appear. (Sometimes the copy shows up right on top of the original, so you may not see it at first.) Now you can move the copied shape or line if you want it to go someplace else.

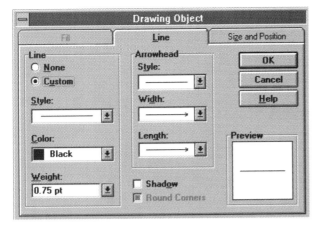

The Line Style dialog box

box choices to change the thickness of your line. Click on the down arrow next to the boxes to see different choices. You can also put arrowheads on your lines using the Style, Width, and Length boxes in the Arrowhead box. Try selecting different choices to see what happens to your line—you can see the changes in the Preview box. Click on the OK button when you're done.

5 Now let's put some patterns inside your shapes. Click on the Selection Tool button, then use the Selection Tool to click on one of your shapes. Go to the Format menu and select the Drawing Object command. This time, click on the Fill tab. You will see the Fill dialog box.

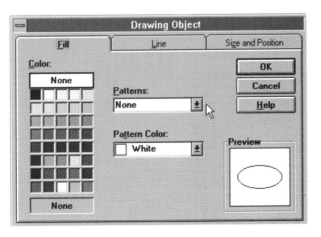

Try This

You can change the way the lines around your shapes look, too. Just select the shape, then select the Drawing Object command from the Format menu. Click on the Line tab, pick a line style, and your shape will have a different line around its edges.

Neat Trick

You can make your squares and rectangles have rounded corners. Open the Line Style dialog box. Then just click the Rounded Corners box so a black *x* shows up. If you want to go back to regular corners, click in the box again to make the *x* disappear.

Sometimes a filled shape will cover up other shapes and lines. Here's how you can choose which shapes and lines are in front and which are in back. Select a shape or line, then look for the buttons with the yellow and black squares down at the bottom of the screen. The one on the left is the Bring to Front button, the one on the right is the Send to Back button. As you might guess, the Bring to Front button will put your shape or line in front of everything else, and the Send to Back button will put your shape or line behind everything else. Just click on either button to use it.

Oh No!

I Want to Change the Color!

To change a color, just click on another colored square. If you don't want any color at all, click on *None.*

To add a pattern, click on the down arrow next to the white box below the word *Pattern.* Then, click on one of the patterns (you may want to use the up and down arrows to move through the list). Next, click on the OK button. Ta da! Your shape is now filled with a pattern. Try picking different patterns for different shapes. If you don't like the pattern you pick, just choose *None* from the pattern choices. Your pattern will go away.

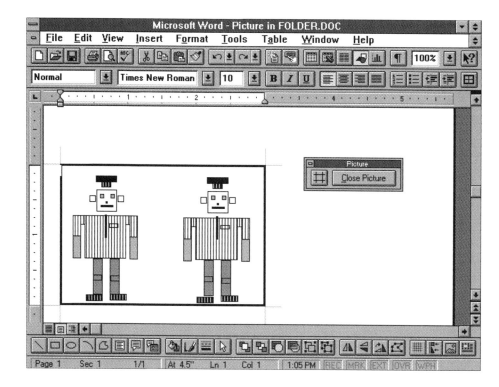

6 Here's a way to change the color of your shapes and lines. Click on the Selection Tool button, then click on a shape or line to select it. Then look at the buttons at the bottom of the window. The one that looks like a paint bucket is the Fill Color button—it changes the color of your shapes. The one that looks like a paint-brush is the Line Color button—it changes the color of your lines. Click on one of the buttons and you'll see a bunch of different-colored squares. Just click on one of the squares to change the color. (Remember, even if you have color in your picture, it won't show up when you print unless you have a color printer.)

7 Play around with your picture until you're happy with it. Then find the tiny window that holds the Close Picture button. Click on the button. The Microsoft Picture window will close, and you'll see your drawing in your Word window.

8 Now let's add some words to your folder. Press the Enter or Return key five or six times so your words will show up below the picture. Think about what you want to write on your folder, then type in the words. Change the size and style of the words if you want. (See the Bumper Stickers project if you want to know more about this.) Then center both the picture and the words—just select them both, and click on the Center Alignment button (or press the Ctrl key and E at the same time). When you're done, save your folder and print it out.

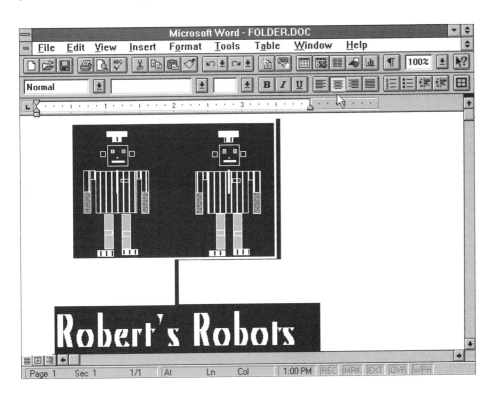

9 If you wish, color in the picture you made for your folder. To add sparkle to your picture, try using some glitter. (If you use glitter, make sure it's dry before going on to step 10.)

10 Put your printed sheet face down with the printed part on the left. Measure 4 inches up from the bottom and make a pencil mark at each side. Fold up the paper from the bottom until the corners of the part you're folding match up with the pencil marks you made. Crease the paper at the fold. This will be your pocket.

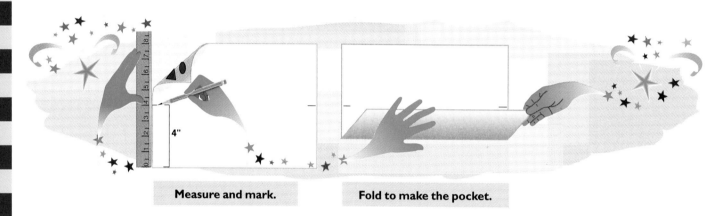

Measure and mark.

Fold to make the pocket.

11 Measure 1 inch in from each corner along the top and bottom, and mark the points. Fold the paper on one side until the corners reach the marks you made on that side. Do the same for the other side. Then glue down the folds. (At the bottom, where the fold crosses the pocket, the paper is double thick, and you'll need to glue down both parts). Let the glue dry.

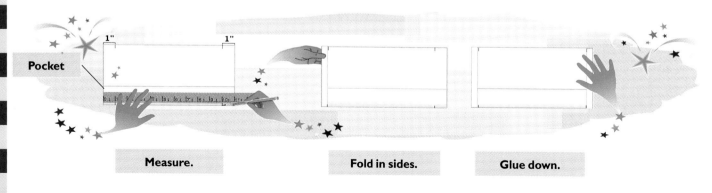

Measure.

Fold in sides.

Glue down.

12 Fold the pocket folder in half across, with the pocket on the inside. Then open it up again. Measure 1 inch on each side of the center fold at the top edge of the pocket (not the top edge of the folder) and draw a diagonal line from each mark to the center fold at the bottom edge of the pocket. Cut along each line to make a triangular notch. Now your pocket folder is ready to stuff!

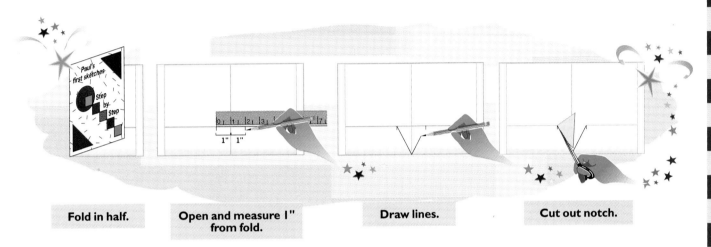

Fold in half.

Open and measure 1" from fold.

Draw lines.

Cut out notch.

Terrific Treasure Chests

These treasure chests are great for storing all sorts of treasures— rocks and shells, photographs, bird feathers, marble collections, or anything else you want to keep in a special place.

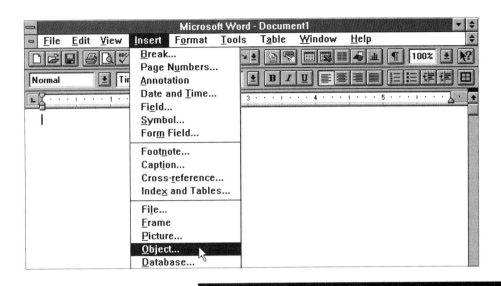

Additional Program: Microsoft Picture

Freeform Tool

- *shoebox with a lid*
- *scissors*
- *glue stick or glue*
- *solid colored paper or construction paper*
- *markers, crayons, or colored pencils*
- *2 large brass paper fasteners*
- *a thumbtack, pushpin, or small nail*
- *colored rubber band*

Continued on next page.

Here's How to Do It

1 We're going to use Microsoft Picture to make special decorations for your treasure chest. To make the first decoration, select the Object command from the Insert menu. Click on the Create New tab, then select *Microsoft Word 6.0 Picture* from the list of names that appears. Click on the OK button. Now you're ready to draw.

2 See the button five in from the left at the bottom that looks like a squiggly line? That's the Freeform Tool button. You can use it to

- *Microsoft Picture (This program comes with Word for Windows. If Microsoft Picture is not present, ask a grown-up to use the Word for Windows disks to install it.)*

make different kinds of lines. Here's what you do. Click on the Freeform Tool button. Then move the pointer inside the gray Boundary box. Hold down the mouse button, and move the mouse around to draw a squiggly line.

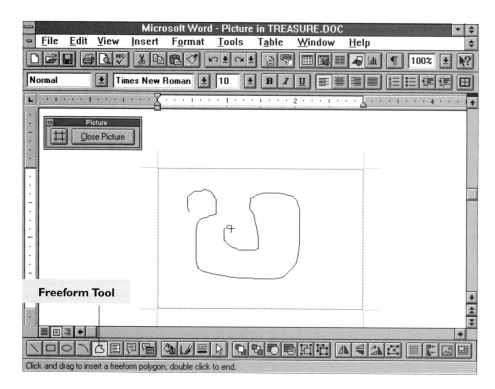

When you want to stop drawing the line, double-click the mouse button. Some small black squares will show up around your line, but don't worry about them—they just show that your line is selected. They'll disappear when you draw another line.

3 You can also use the Freeform Tool to make lines that have both straight and curvy parts. To do this, start by drawing a line as you did in step 2. Then, while you're drawing, let go of the mouse button, but still move the mouse. You'll see a straight line that changes size as the mouse moves. If you want to make a corner, just click once and then move the mouse again to make the straight line go in a different direction. To make the next part of the line curvy again, just press and hold the mouse button as you move the mouse.

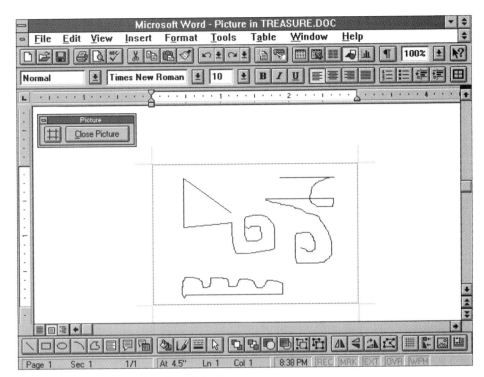

Combinations of curved and straight lines

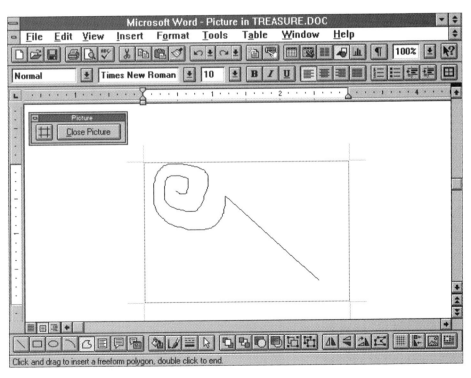

A curved and straight line

Oh No!

I Don't Like My Line!

If you don't like something you've drawn, just select it using the Selection Tool, then select the Cut command from the Edit menu, or use the Delete key.

Neat Trick

Microsoft Picture lets you flip or rotate your shapes and lines. First use the Selection Tool to select the shape or line you want to change. Then look for the buttons that have two triangles on them (they're the sixth, seventh, and eighth buttons in from the right). The one with the two upright triangles is the Flip Horizontal button, the one with the two sideways triangles is the Flip Vertical button, and the one with one upright and one sideways triangle is the Rotate button. Just click on the one you want to use.

Try holding down and letting go of the mouse button at different times to see what kinds of lines you can make. When you're done with each line, double click the mouse button to finish the line.

4 Draw a picture using the Freeform Tool. If you want, use the other shape tools as well. You can also use the Drawing Object command in the Format menu to change the things you draw. (For more about drawing and changing shapes and lines, see the Pen and Pencil Holders and Mini Pocket Folders projects.)

5 Once you have a picture you like, click on the Close Picture button (it's in the tiny Picture window). You'll return to the regular Word window.

6 Now, let's make a second picture. Make sure that the insertion point (the blinking line) is to the right of your picture. Then press the Enter or Return key three or four times. Select the Object command from the Insert menu again. Then select *Microsoft Word 6.0 Picture* from the list of names that appears, and click on the OK button. Now you're ready to draw another picture. When you're done with your second picture, click on the Close Picture button.

7 Make a few more pictures, adding them the same way you did in step 6.

8 Now you can make your pictures different sizes, if you want. To do this, click on one of your pictures to select it. You'll see a border with some small black squares along the edges. Move the pointer over the square in the lower-right corner until the pointer turns into a diagonal line with an arrow on each end. Hold down the mouse button, then move the mouse. You'll see a dotted rectangle that moves as you move the mouse.

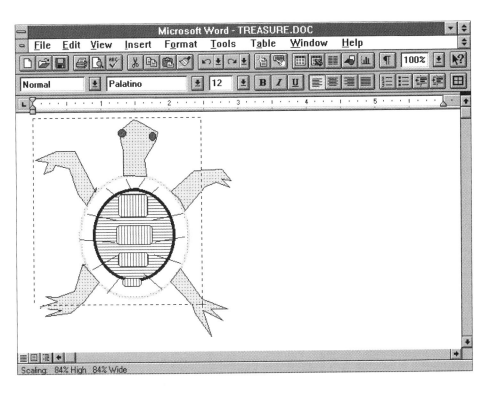

The dotted rectangle shows you the new size your picture will be. If you want the picture smaller, move the mouse so the rectangle is smaller; if you want your picture larger, then move the mouse so the rectangle is bigger. When the rectangle is the size you want, let go of the mouse button. Your picture will be the new size.

9 Save your pictures and print them out.(If you need help, see Saving Your Files, page 3, and Printing Tips, page 5.) You may want to print out several copies so you have enough pictures for your treasure chest.

10 Now you're ready to decorate your treasure chest. Cut out pieces of colored paper big enough to cover up any printing that's on the shoebox or its lid, and glue down.

Try This

You can also use colored paper or gift wrap to line the inside of your treasure chest. Place the shoebox on top of the paper and trace around the bottom. Then move the shoebox to another part of the paper, turn it on one side, and trace around the side. Do this for the other sides as well. Cut out the paper around the traced lines, and glue the pieces onto the inside sides and bottom. Trim or fold each piece to fit.

11 Color the pictures you printed. Then cut them out. (If your picture is an odd shape that's hard to cut out, just leave a box or circle around it.) Glue your pictures to the sides and lid of the shoebox.

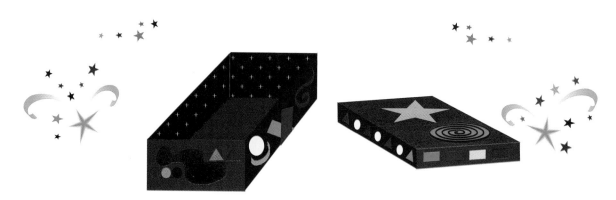

12 To make a flap for the lid of the chest, cut the shoebox lid at each corner of one of the long sides.

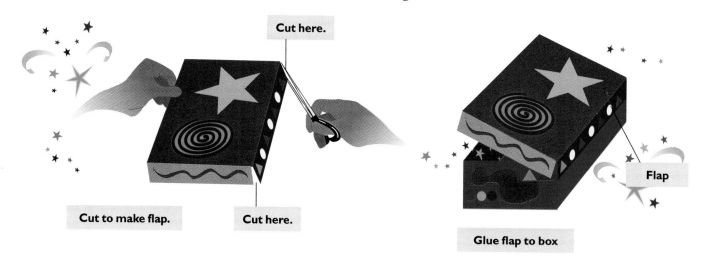

Cut here.

Cut to make flap.

Cut here.

Flap

Glue flap to box

Put glue on the inside of the flap. Then, put the lid on the shoe box and press along the flap to glue it down. You may want to lay it on its side, with the glue side down, while it's drying.

Watch Out!

Make sure your fingers are out of the way when you push in the tack to make the hole.

13 Use the thumbtack to make a small hole in the center of the side of the shoe box opposite to the flap. Make the hole closer to the bottom than to the top. Put in one of the brass fasteners. (You can make the hole larger with a pencil point if you need to.)

Make another small hole—this time in the edge of the lid—that lines up with the hole you made in the box. Put the second fastener in this hole.

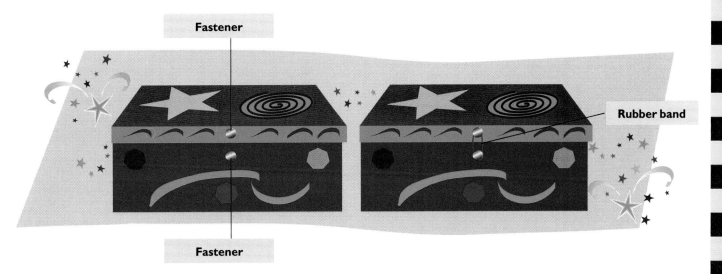

Fastener

Fastener

Rubber band

14 Now you can fasten your box by looping a rubber band around the fasteners. If your rubber band is very long, just loop it around two or three times until it's tight. To open the treasure chest, just take off the rubber band and lift the lid.

Silly Stickers

Everyone loves stickers...and now you can make your own! These stickers can be as silly or as serious as you want.

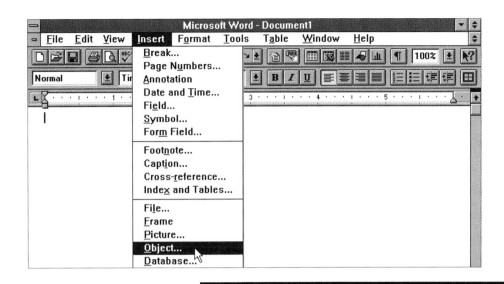

Text Box Tool

Reset Boundary button

Here's How to Do It

1 Let's start out by making a picture for your sticker. Select the Object command from the Insert menu. When the Object Dialog box appears, click on the Create New tab at the top. Then, select *Microsoft Word 6.0 Picture* from the list of names and click on the OK button.

2 Use the different shape and line tools to make a picture. (If you don't know how to use the tools, see the Pen and Pencil Holders and Terrific Treasure Chests projects.) Try filling in the shapes and lines you make using the

You'll Need

- *markers, crayons, or colored pencils*
- *glue stick or glue*
- *clear contact paper*
- *scissors*
- *Microsoft Picture (This program comes with Word for Windows. If Microsoft Picture is not present, ask a grown-up to use the Word for Windows disks to install it.)*

Drawing Object command in the Format menu. (To find out more about this command, see the Mini Pocket Folders project.)

3 Let's add some words to your sticker. To do this, you'll use the Text Box Tool to draw boxes for your words. Click on the Text Box Tool button (it's six in from the left). The Text Box Tool works like the Rectangle Tool—just move the pointer back over to your picture, hold down the mouse button, and drag. When your text box is the size you want it to be, let go of the mouse button. You'll see a gray border around the text box and a blinking line (the insertion point) inside the box. Just type in your name or even a silly slogan.

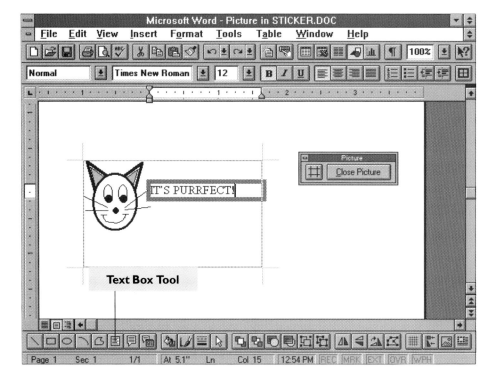

Text Box Tool

4 Now we can change the way the words look. Just use the mouse to select all the words in the box. Then use the regular Font box, Point Size box, Style buttons, and Alignment buttons to make changes. (If you need to know more

about these things, see the Bumper Stickers and Party Placemats projects.)

5 If you want, you can change the pattern inside the text box as well as the lines around it the same way you change the pattern and lines of a rectangle. Use the Selection Tool to select the text box. Then select the Drawing Object command from the Format menu. If you want to change the pattern, click on the Fill tab. If you want to change the lines, click on the Lines tab. Make the changes you want, then click on the OK button. (If you need help using the Drawing Object command, see steps 4 and 5 of the Mini Pocket Folders project.)

6 You can also move your words around to different places. Select your text box using the Selection Tool so the gray border shows up around the words. Then point to the middle of the text box, hold down the mouse button, and move the mouse. The text box will move as the mouse moves. Let go of the mouse button when your words are in the right place.

Oh No!

When I Make Changes, Some of My Words Disappear!

If this happens, your text box is too small. To make it larger, click on the Selection Tool, then click on the text box to make the gray border with the small black squares (the handles) appear. Put the pointer over one of the handles, hold down the mouse button, and drag the mouse. The text box will change size as you move the mouse. When the text box is large enough to see all of your words, let go of the mouse button.

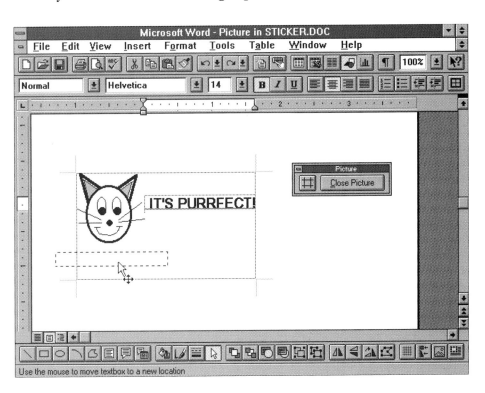

7 Play around with your picture until you like it. Now let's make it so there won't be a lot of white space around your finished sticker. You can do this by changing the Boundary box (the gray lines in the Picture window) so it fits exactly around your picture and words. All you need to do is click on the Reset Boundary button (it's next to the Close Picture button in the tiny Picture window). See how the gray lines now fit around your picture?

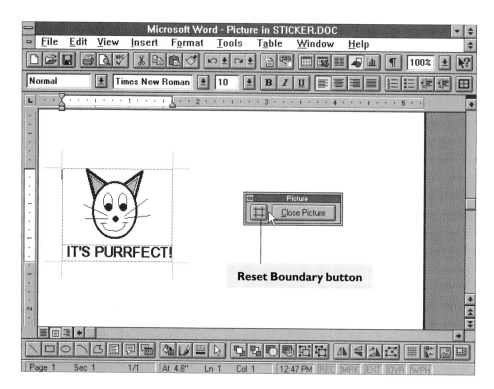

8 When your picture is done, click on the Close Picture button to get back to the regular Word window.

9 Let's add a border around your sticker so you'll be able to cut it out later. Select the picture by clicking on it. Then go to the Format menu and select the Borders and Shading command. When the Borders and Shading dialog box appears, click on the Borders tab.

Next click on the middle box under the word *Presets*. Then click on one of the different line styles under the word *Style* on the right side. You'll see what your border will look like in the Border box on the left side. When you've decided on the line style you like, click on the OK button.

10 Now we'll make copies of your sticker, so you can put it all over! Click on the picture again to select it. Then select the Copy command from the Edit menu. Next, click outside your picture on the right side. Then choose Paste from the Edit menu. Another copy of your sticker will appear.

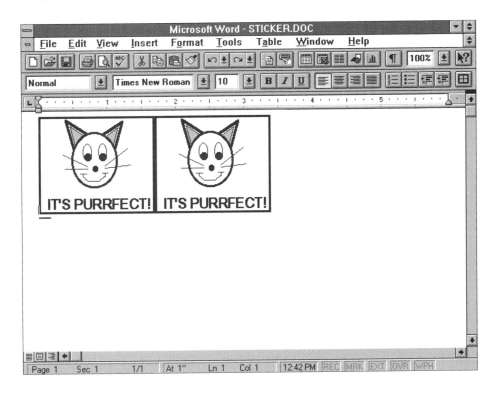

11 Make as many copies as you want, by using the Paste command over and over again. Then save your picture and print it out. (For more on saving and printing, see Saving Your Files, page 3, and Printing Tips, page 5.)

Try This

If you have sticker paper for your printer, print out your stickers using the sticker paper. Then all you have to do is color them in, cut them apart, and stick them up!

12 Color in your stickers with markers, crayons, or colored pencils. Then, turn over your sheet of stickers and put glue all over the back. Make sure the back of each sticker is completely covered. (You can probably see the outline of the pictures through the back of the sheet.)

13 Glue the whole sheet of stickers to the front side of a piece of contact paper. Remember, you want to glue the stickers to the shiny part of the contact paper, not to the backing or sticky part. Put a heavy book on top of your stickers while they dry, so they'll stay flat.

Contact paper, shiny side up

Backing

Peel off backing to use.

Stickers

Glue stickers to contact paper.

Cut out when dry.

14 When the glue is dry, cut out each sticker around its border. When you're ready to use a sticker, just peel off the contact paper backing and press it down!

Perfect Pop-Ups

Want to surprise a friend or someone in your family? Give them one of these special greeting cards. When you open the card, the picture pops up!

YOU'RE THE TOPS!

It's Your Birthday!

Jump for Joy!

TO: DAD   LOVE: DANIEL

HAPPY VALENTINE'S DAY!

On the Menu

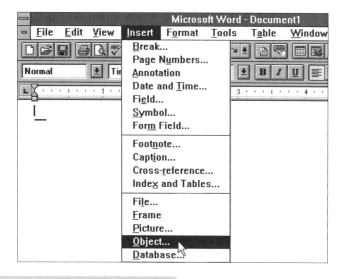

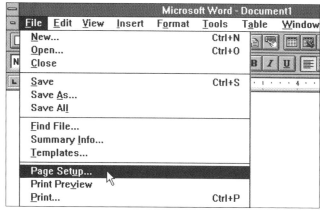

You'll Need

- *ruler*
- *pencil*
- *scissors*
- *markers, crayons, or colored pencils*
- *glue stick or glue*
- *8½-by-11-inch piece of paper, any color*
- *Microsoft Picture (This program comes with Word for Windows. If Microsoft Picture is not present, ask a grown-up to use the Word for Windows disks to install it.)*

Here's How to Do It

1 First we'll set the margins of the page, so the print will be in the right place when you fold the card. Here's what you need to do: Go to the File menu and select Page Setup. When the Page Setup dialog box appears, click on the Margins tab. Find the white box next to the word *Top*, and change the number in it to **6.5** (use a period for the dot between the 6 and the 5). Then click on the OK button.

2 Decide what type of card you want to make. Will it be a birthday card? A congratulations card? Maybe a Mother's Day or Father's Day card? Type in the words that you want to appear inside your card. Change the typeface (the font), the typesize (the point size), and the style and alignment of the type, if you wish. (If you need help doing this, see the Bumper Stickers and Party Placemats projects.)

3 Now we're going to center your words between the top and bottom of the folded page. To do this, go to the File menu and select Page Setup again. This time, click on the Layout tab. You'll see a dialog box like this:

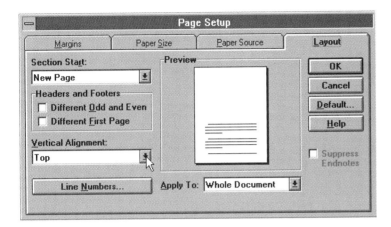

Click on the down arrow next to the Vertical Alignment box. Then click on the word *Center* from the choices that appear. Click on the OK button. (You won't see anything change, but don't worry—the words are now centered vertically.)

4 Now let's add the art, using Microsoft Picture. You'll need a new page for this, but you don't have to open a new file. Instead, you can tell Word to start a new page whenever you want it. First, click at the end of the last word you typed. Then press Enter once. Now go to the Insert menu and select the Break command. When the Break dialog box appears, click in the circle next to the words *Page Break*. Then click on the OK button. You'll see a line with the words *Page Break* in the middle. This line doesn't print. It just shows you where one page ends and the next one begins.

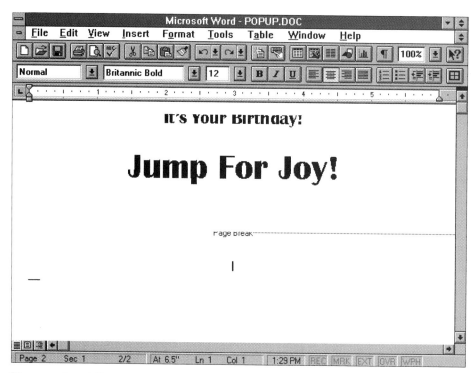

The page-break line

You can also type in a message for the outside of the card. Just add another page break, as you did in step 4. Then type in the words. You don't have to tell Word to center your message vertically, because it remembers that you've already done this.

5 Next, select the Object command from the Insert menu, and click on the Create New tab. Click on the words *Microsoft Word 6.0 Picture*, then click on the OK button. The Picture window will appear. Use the different tools to make a drawing for your card. (See the Pen and Pencil Holders, Mini Pocket Folders, and Terrific Treasure Chests projects if you need to know more about Picture.) When you like your picture, click on the Close Picture button.

6 Save your work and print it out. (If you need help with printing and saving, see Saving Your Files, page 3, and Printing Tips, page 5.)

7 Now let's put your card together. Fold the page that has the inside message in half across, with the print on the inside. Measure along the folded edge, and make a mark 3¾ inches from the side. Then make another mark 4¾ inches from the same side. Draw a line 1-inch long straight down from each mark.

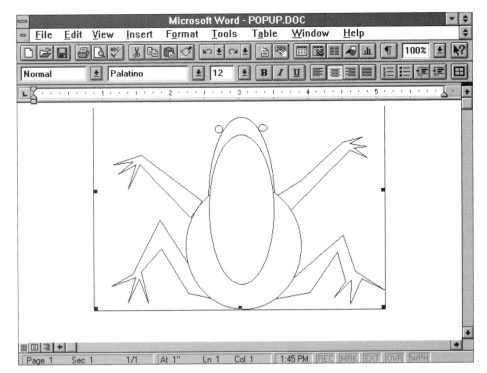

A drawing for the pop-up card

Try This

You can make your card really fancy by printing out each page on a different color of paper.

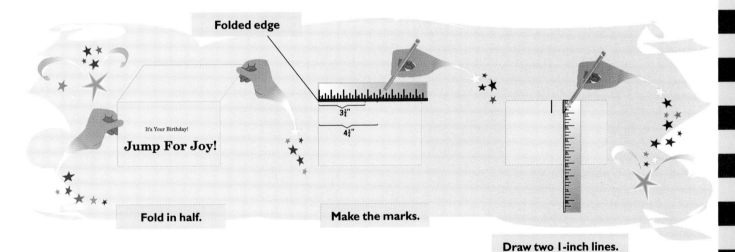

Folded edge

It's Your Birthday!

Jump For Joy!

$3\frac{3}{4}$"

$4\frac{3}{4}$"

Fold in half.

Make the marks.

Draw two 1-inch lines.

8 Cut along the two 1-inch-long lines. When you unfold the page, there will be two slits in the middle. Push the strip of paper between the slits in from the back and crease it up in the opposite direction of the fold, so it makes a little step. Then crease the step at the top and the bottom so when you fold the paper, the step stays on the inside, and the outside has a rectangular notch.

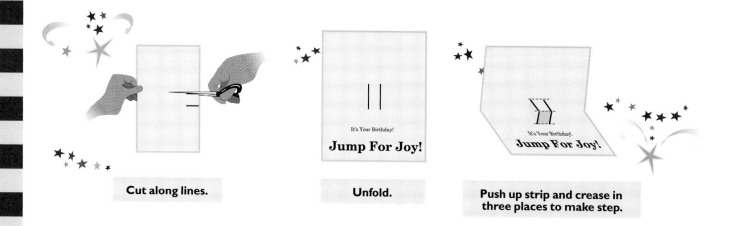

Cut along lines.

Unfold.

**Push up strip and crease in
three places to make step.**

9 Color the picture you made, if you wish, then cut it out. Glue it to the front side of the step, facing the printed message. When the glue is dry, fold the page back up. There should still be a notch in the folded side.

Glue picture to front of step.

Try This

You can add a background scene to your pop-up card by coloring in the top inside page.

10 Fold the paper for the outside of the card in half across. (If you have a message on this page, make sure the print is on the outside.) Make a crease at the fold. Then unfold the paper.

11 Now put glue all over one half of the folded, notched page (the outside of the inside message page). But don't put any glue on the notch! Glue it to one side of the outside page, matching the fold to the crease and lining up the edges. Then put glue on the other half of the folded, notched page. Fold down the outside page over it and smooth them together, lining up the edges.

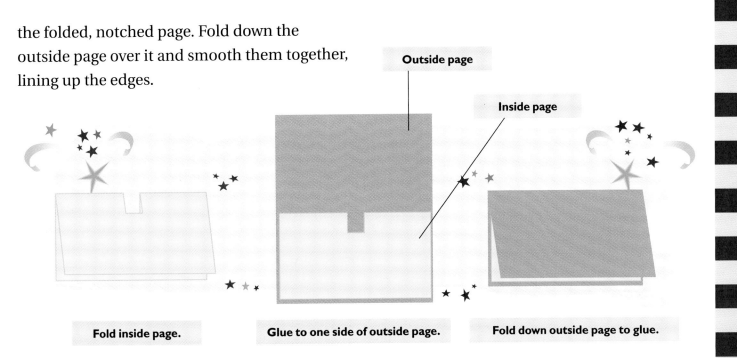

Fold inside page.

Glue to one side of outside page.

Fold down outside page to glue.

12 Let the glue dry. Then decorate the outside of the card with markers, crayons, or colored pencils. When you unfold the card, the picture pops up!

Watch Out

Make sure the printed messages on both pages will be right side up when the whole card is folded.

Index

Imagination.
Innovation. Insight.

The How It Works Series from Ziff-Davis Press

"... a magnificently seamless integration of text and graphics ..."

Larry Blasko, The Associated Press, reviewing *PC/Computing How Computers Work*

No other books bring computer technology to life like the *How It Works* series from Ziff-Davis Press. Lavish, full-color illustrations and lucid text from some of the world's top computer commentators make *How It Works* books an exciting way to explore the inner workings of PC technology.

ISBN: 094-7 Price: $22.95

PC/Computing How Computers Work

A worldwide blockbuster that hit the general trade bestseller lists! *PC/Computing* magazine executive editor Ron White dismantles the PC and reveals what really makes it tick.

How Networks Work

Two of the most respected names in connectivity showcase the PC network, illustrating and explaining how each component does its magic and how they all fit together.

ISBN: 129-3 Price: $24.95

How Macs Work

A fun and fascinating voyage to the heart of the Macintosh! Two noted *MacUser* contributors cover the spectrum of Macintosh operations from startup to shutdown.

How Software Works

This dazzlingly illustrated volume from Ron White peeks inside the PC to show in full-color how software breathes life into the PC. Covers Windows™ and all major software categories.

ISBN: 133-1 Price: $24.95

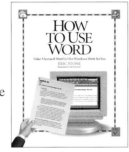

HOW TO USE WORD

Make Microsoft Word 6.0 for Windows Work for You

ERIC STONE

ISBN: 184-6 Price: $17.95

HOW MACS WORK

JOHN RIZZO AND K. DANIEL CLARK

ISBN: 146-3 Price: $24.95

How to Use Your Computer

Conquer computerphobia and see how this intricate machine truly makes life easier. Dozens of full-color graphics showcase the components of the PC and explain how to interact with them.

All About Computers

This one-of-a-kind visual guide for kids features numerous full-color illustrations and photos on every page, combined with dozens of interactive projects that reinforce computer basics, making this an exciting way to learn all about the world of computers.

How To Use Word

Make Word 6.0 for Windows Work for You!

A uniquely visual approach puts the basics of Microsoft's latest Windows-based word processor right before the reader's eyes. Colorful examples invite them to begin producing a variety of documents, quickly and easily. Truly innovative!

How To Use Excel

Make Excel 5.0 for Windows Work for You!

Covering the latest version of Excel, this visually impressive resource guides beginners to spreadsheet fluency through a full-color graphical approach that makes powerful techniques seem plain as day. Hands-on "Try It" sections give new users a chance to sharpen newfound skills.

HOW TO USE YOUR COMPUTER

LISA BIOW

ISBN: 155-2 Price: $22.95

ALL ABOUT COMPUTERS

JEAN ATELSEK

DISCOVER THE WORLD OF COMPUTERS

ISBN: 166-8 Price: $15.95

HOW TO USE EXCEL

Make Excel 5.0 for Windows Work for You

ERIC STONE

ISBN: 185-4 Price: $17.95

Available at all fine bookstores or by calling 1-800-688-0448, ext. 100. Call for more information on the Instructor's Supplement, including transparencies for each book in the *How It Works* Series.

ZIFF-DAVIS
ZD
PRESS

© 1993 Ziff-Davis Press

The Quick and Easy Way to Learn.

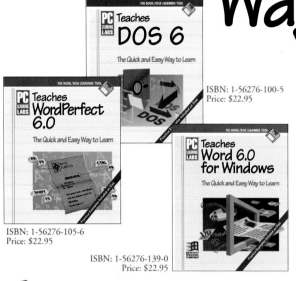

ISBN: 1-56276-100-5
Price: $22.95

ISBN: 1-56276-105-6
Price: $22.95

ISBN: 1-56276-139-0
Price: $22.95

We know that PC Learning Labs books are the fastest and easiest way to learn because years have been spent perfecting them. Beginners will find practice sessions that are easy to follow and reference information that is easy to find. Even the most computer-shy readers can gain confidence faster than they ever thought possible.

The time we spent designing this series translates into time saved for you. You can feel confident that the information is accurate and presented in a way that allows you to learn quickly and effectively.

ISBN: 1-56276-122-6
Price: $22.95

ISBN: 1-56276-176-5
Price: $22.95

ISBN: 1-56276-148-X
Price: $22.95

ISBN: 1-56276-135-8
Price: $22.95

ISBN: 1-56276-020-3
Price: $22.95

ISBN: 1-56276-134-X
Price: $22.95

ISBN: 1-56276-124-2
Price: $22.95

ISBN: 1-56276-074-2
Price: $22.95

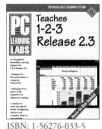

ISBN: 1-56276-033-5
Price: $22.95

ISBN: 1-56276-051-3
Price: $22.95

ISBN: 1-56276-154-4
Price: $22.95

ISBN: 1-56276-138-2
Price: $22.95

Also available: Titles featuring new versions of Excel, 1-2-3, Access, Microsoft Project, Ami Pro, and new applications, pending software release. Call 1-800-688-0448 for title update information.

Available at all fine bookstores, or by calling 1-800-688-0448, ext. 103.

ZIFF-DAVIS
ZD
PRESS